BUDDHISM

*Beginner's Guide to Understanding &
Practicing Buddhism to Become Stress
and Anxiety Free*

TABLE OF CONTENTS

INTRODUCTION

Do you know that Buddhism is more popular now than it was half a century ago?

You can tell, based on the surge of books written about it as well as the increase in the number of Buddhist and Yoga schools, throughout the globe, notably in the west. You might even have noticed more people – from movie stars to athletes, your next-door neighbor to millionaire tycoons – who are incorporating such Buddhist practices as meditation into their everyday lives.

However, many of the common questions about Buddhism remain unanswered. For instance, is it some sort of religion with its own rigid set of rules? Is it a carefree type of lifestyle? What is reincarnation? Is karma similar to fate?

If you are curious to know the answers, and if you want to learn more about Buddhism, especially with regard to becoming stress and anxiety-free, then this book was written especially for you!

It is no secret that Buddhism is a complex topic. After all, the seed that the First Buddha planted almost three thousand years ago is now a massive tree that continues to branch out to this day. Nevertheless, this book can help you build a strong foundation for learning and practicing Buddhism.

All the fundamental questions asked by beginners are answered here, such as what Buddhism is and what its teachings are. Core subjects such as the Four Noble Truths and the Noble Eightfold Path are described clearly. Buddhist concepts such as Reincarnation, Nirvana, and Karma are also explained in a clear and concise way. Theories aside, you will also learn the practical side of Buddhism, specifically to help you achieve peace and relaxation each day.

1

This book is for anybody who is curious about Buddhism, particularly those who are considering it as their guide to a happy and purposeful life.

Now, the choice is yours. Clear the fog and begin your spiritual journey towards attaining peace of mind and clarity. The First Chapter awaits you!

A MIND UNPERTURBED BY THE VAGARIES OF FORTUNE, FROM SORROW, FREED, FROM DEFILEMENTS CLEANSED, FROM FEAR LIBERATED - THIS IS THE GREATEST BLESSING

CHAPTER 1

WHAT IS BUDDHISM?

"A mind unperturbed by the vagaries of fortune, from sorrow, freed, from defilements cleansed, from fear liberated — this is the greatest blessing."

— The Buddha

Hello! You must be the kind of person who is eager to learn new things every day. After all, why else would you choose this book?

You must be curious about Buddhism. You might have heard of it from somewhere, such as on social media or from a friend who is passionate about its teachings.

You might also have heard about the many ways it has helped those who find their true purpose in life, or – at the very least – find peace and calm in the midst of a seemingly fast-paced and stressful world.

A million questions might be swimming in your brain concerning Buddhism. In a while, they will be answered.

First, do take comfort in being here right now: reading this book and

3

acquiring the knowledge that can help you find true happiness in everyday life.

One of the most essential teachings of Buddhism is an understanding that where you are at this moment is exactly where you are intended to be. As each moment passes, you are following your own course throughout life and enjoying and taking in each moment is paramount in creating a path of wisdom and understanding for yourself. Revel in each and every sentence, taking the time to fully understand what you are reading because, in Buddhism, every tale, every reading, and every teaching pave the way to a more open, joyful and enlightened path in life.

Look around you and notice how your body has naturally kept you alive. Your lungs continue to breathe without you having to tell them to do so. Your eyelids blink automatically to keep your eyes moist and protected. Your blood continues to flow underneath your skin, oblivious to your surroundings and thoughts.

Also, notice how you are able to comprehend the words on this page. Is that not something to be grateful for? Take a moment to consider this thought.

Are you still here? Hopefully yes, because now let us answer what may be the first question in your mind: What is Buddhism?

What is Buddhism?

Would it surprise you to know that Buddhism is not a religion? At least, not in the sense wherein it is an institution that dictates how one should believe in a divine power. Many people make that mistake and avoid Buddhism because they believe it to be contrary to the teachings of their church. However, you can practice Buddhism in conjunction with your personal belief and religion, or as a complement to it.

In fact, there is no deity to be worshipped, although you might wonder why some seem to be worshipping the statues of the Buddha. While there indeed are those who worship his image (and erroneously so), true Buddhists merely pay respect to the memory of the Buddha. They neither worship nor pray to him. The Buddha himself is a guide and teacher for those that seek the path to enlightenment. The altars that you see in a Buddhist temple are inspirational and remind Buddhists of the path that they have chosen to walk. The colors of the decoration of a Buddhist temple are indeed made up of colors that are easily seen by the eye and the Buddha statue is there as a guide to your meditative process.

Many people who wake up each morning with the intention of practicing Buddhist teachings find inspiration from the gentle image of the Buddha. It is not unlike finding your motivation from the words of a successful person. His peaceful and meditative image can help you understand and remember the teachings you are following when life becomes stressful, and your mind begins to run off course. Thus, it follows that creating a meditative area and adorning it with a Buddha statue or other inspirational items is common for westerners.

Buddhism is a way of life that leads to the discernment of true reality. Its teachings center on developing your ability to be mindful of your thoughts, actions, and surroundings. All these lead to a life that is in tune with nature and your true self. You may find it hard to understand at first, but everything that happens in your life is dictated by your thoughts and when you meditate, you get a clearer look at what needs to change in your world, as well as learning more about who you are in relation to the world that you live in or even the body that you inhabit.

The practices of Buddhism – including meditation and yoga – are meant to help you unlearn your preconceived notions of yourself and the world. They serve as your guide towards embracing such qualities as kindness, love, true wisdom, and awareness. Over the course of our youth, we are taught society values and these may not run in line with true values which is why this reminder is needed. Look at the uncertainty in the world, and at the bottom of it, you will always find a line of thought that leads you to the unhappiness that you experience. This may be biased toward certain members of society or it may indeed be a lack of self-worth brought on by your interaction with society.

Those who continually walk the path of Buddhism usually find themselves achieving the state of "perfect enlightenment." In other words, they become a "Buddha." A Buddha is a being who has been able to see the nature of life as it truly is. The enlightened being then continues to live life fully, all the while upholding the principles that are in line with this vision. Since this philosophy may question your current motivation, your beliefs and your way of life, you need to be open-minded enough to learn because the teachings are very thorough. To reach enlightenment, you need to be able to let go of values that may at

5

the current time be fundamental to who you are.

The idea of enlightenment can be broken down into two simple forms, the mind, and the self. The mind is that constant voice that has been molded and constructed based on the world around you in this life. Self is that inner being that is separate from the meat of your body and does not change based on any teachings or experiences that life brings you. Your real self is what can be understood to travel from life to life during reincarnation. In different belief systems, these are given names, such as the soul, though what name you give it isn't important. It is merely important that you recognize that these two parts of you exist and that, if you are unhappy in your life, the harmony or balance is missing and that's where Buddhism helps you to align these values so that both parts of you are in harmony with each other.

Each and every living being has the opportunity to become enlightened in each life they live. There is no set course or prewritten script for your life. As discussed later in this book, Karma plays a part in deciding the circumstances in which you will be born into from life to life, but your own spiritual and mental ambition are what drives each person to take one step closer to full enlightenment.

However, things get interesting here, because when you follow the path of Buddhism, you do not have an "end goal." It is a paradox for one to declare that they are going to practice Buddhism in order to reach enlightenment.

Who is The Buddha?

The word "Buddha" translates to "the enlightened one" or "the awakened being." It refers to any being who has achieved this state. However, you might be curious to know about the first Buddha.

According to legend, the first Buddha was named Siddhartha Gautama. Many believe that he was born around 563 B.C. in a land that is now found in Nepal. It is said that The Buddha was born a royal, shielded from the suffering of the kingdom of his father, who built a grand palace around him void of religion or human suffering. The King created an entire world inside those castle walls and, as his son grew, led him to believe that the world was one of happiness, empathy, and joy. The King was told by seers when the prince was born that he would either be a great warrior or a spiritual leader.

Later in his life, after he had married and was raised, he ventured out into the world and saw the truth of humanity. He met an old man and found that all people age, and eventually die.

At the age of twenty-nine, he found that neither his power nor his fortune brought him true happiness, and he wanted to understand the world outside of the palace walls.

Therefore, what he did was he set out to explore as many religions across the world as he could to find the answer to the question that we all ask ourselves, "Where can one find happiness?" He tried many ways including fasting and when he found that fasting was not helping him in the way that he thought it might, he decided to meditate on the problems that he faced. While others still practiced going without food and had thought that Siddhartha had given up the practice, he had in fact taken himself on another route – one that would lead him to enlightenment.

Several years into his spiritual pilgrimage, the Buddha discovered "The Middle Path" while meditating under the Bodhi tree. This path is a way of balance, not of extremism, which he found only through trial and error. He sat for days under that Bodhi tree seeking the answers he had initially set out to find. During this meditation, Siddhartha had to face the evil demon known as Mara, who threatened to stand in the way of his Buddha status. He looked to the earth for guidance and the land answered by banishing Mara and allowing Siddhartha to reach full enlightenment. Such discernment led him to achieve the perfect state of enlightenment. After this life-changing experience, the Buddha then lived the rest of his days sharing what he had discovered. The followers of the Buddha's teachings called his principles the *Dharma*, or "Truth."

It is thought that Buddha or anyone who reaches the state of perfect enlightenment in their lifetime no longer continues on the circle of rebirth. Instead, the Buddha is thought to sit outside of constant reincarnation and sends teachings and guidance to those searching for their own freedom of self. They no longer have to sit through what Buddhists believe to be an endless cycle of suffering known as life.

When you hear the word suffering, you may have images of pain and anger come into your mind, but in Buddhism, they believe that all life is suffering. As humans, we feel the pain of loss, the emotions of sadness, happiness, disappointment, and so on. These emotions are manifestations of our mind, and they do not come from our inner selves. Because they do not come from our true selves, they are thought of as suffering. These are false feelings created by the meat of our brains, programmed into us by what our societal view has taught us. The way forward was through following the Noble Eightfold Path and this allowed people to be closer to the potential of enlightenment.

Currently, Buddhism is increasingly becoming a popular way of life for millions of people, across the world. Even those in the Western countries seek to follow The Middle Path because they find that it speaks to their heart. There is also the fact that traditional medicines do very little for the status quo. For example, if you are depressed or if you are unable to deal with the feelings that you have, scientists have established that the Buddhist way offers you a better and more permanent solution to your problems. Medical findings that explored the relationship between the Buddhist way and the way that the brain operated found that Buddhist monks were able to simultaneously use the creative side of the brain and the calculating side of the brain and that they were, therefore more open to creativity.

In a world where everything is always in motion, constantly forcing us to move forward at a quicker and more rapid pace, many people feel the loss of their connection with nature. Though nature is all around us, even in the major cities, what we have done to change the pure form of Earth, creates a disconnect from our minds. In Buddhism, you are connected to every natural thing in this world, and by practicing the teachings of it, you are brought back to that connection. This is an enormous draw for millions of people all over the world. You can think of it as connecting back to your roots.

If you are unsure of what this means, you only have to look to see what happens when you go somewhere that you find to be inspiring. The feelings that you experience don't just come from the external stimuli. They come from your inner self-recognizing the joy that lies in that ever moving thing called nature. We celebrate the changing of the seasons and the weather and get up close and personal with nature in an attempt to find ourselves.

Another reason why Buddhism is widespread is the fact that the Buddha never claimed to be a god. Instead, he was a teacher who shared his wisdom based on his own discernment and experiences in life. This lack of an invisible deity often speaks to those that cannot find solace or belief in other religions where God is their governing body. Though there are many tales and teachings in Buddhism, there is no one holy book such as a Bible or Quran. Instead, the "bible" of Buddhism can be found in every natural effect on the planet, from the leaves on the trees to the worms in the ground. They are the story of the past, but you don't need to look to the past to find enlightenment, you need to look at every moment that you experience.

Moreover, the belief system of Buddhism is one that can be described as "large-minded." This means that those who practice it are open to accepting the moral teachings of other belief systems. Therefore, they are unconcerned with labels that pertain to specific religions, such as "Catholic," "Baptist," "Hindu," "Muslim," or even "Buddhist" itself. It is not uncommon to find those of different religious background meditating together at various Buddhist centers, especially in the western world. Enlightenment, in Buddhism, is not based on who you believe created you, but rather by opening your mind enough to allow yourself to shine through. Once that is reached, all the answers you seek on creation will be known to you. Therefore, your title of faith is of no concern, though, those who strive for enlightenment do usually find themselves identifying as Buddhist or other similar namesakes.

Buddhists neither seek an expansion of an organization nor attempt to convince others of a certain belief. Instead, they only provide an explanation if asked. The Buddha encourages one to be curious through awareness; therefore, Buddhism can be regarded more as a way of life-based on discernment rather than faith.

Though Buddhism as a practice can bend and move on a scale depending on your dedication to the teachings and heritage, anyone can practice the Buddhist way of living. There is always an extreme importance put on the word empathy, throughout the teachings of Buddhas through the generations. Empathy is not just reserved for humans, but for every living creature of this world.

At this point, you must be eager to learn the different teachings of the Buddha. Keep in mind that the Buddha's teachings are vast to such an extent that it grew into many different types of Buddhism. These teachings can bring wisdom to anyone, whether seeking to find their true self through enlightenment, or those that just wish to understand the world around them a little bit better. These teachings are for the young and old alike, regardless of religion, status, gender, or heritage.

However, let us not get ahead of ourselves. For now, you can explore more about the teachings of Buddhism, which you can conveniently find in the next chapter. Before you do turn the page, though, please do remember the advice of the Buddha himself. It is to take care not to take his word for it but to test for yourself his teachings. Only by doing so will you then be able to find the true meaning of his words.

You have to discern the truth for yourself because your truth will not be everyone else's. With the constant changes that happen throughout life, the Buddhist belief encourages that you embrace the moment and are ever present in it. For westerners, this is always a little difficult, since we are always striving to better ourselves, although sometimes the betterment that we seek is actually detrimental. You need to read through the next chapters to understand what betterment means. If you were to talk to Tibetans, for example, they do not find merit in people trying to prove that they are better than others. Boasting is not part of the Buddhist way of life which is in contrast to the life in a modern society which encourages competition and heroics that have very little to do with betterment from a Buddhist point of view.

The idea of Siddhartha Gautama was to encourage people to understand that their actions dictate the outcome of different stages of their lives. This is always something that westerners find hard to understand. However, when you see how Buddhist philosophy includes different elements, you will see that the whole picture of your life has been covered and that there are actions you can take to increase your own awareness and your sense of happiness. Our current Dalai Lama was once asked what surprised him the most about mankind and his answer will give you something to think about which relates to modern times and which you can probably identify with. His answer was:

"Man surprised me most about humanity. Because he sacrifices his health in order to make money.
Then he sacrifices money to recuperate his health. And then he is so anxious about the future that he does not enjoy the present; the result being that he does not live in the present or the future; he lives as if he is never going to die, and then dies having never really lived."

The Dalai Lama

When you consider what he is saying, it's plain that all-time at this moment that is spent elsewhere – i.e. either worrying about the future or looking back with regret at the past is time wasted because you then lose the moment that you are in. How many times have you considered something as desperately serious only to find in a short while that you can look back on it and realize that your worries were unfounded?

Mindfulness forms a very important part of the Buddhist philosophy and while you are not present at the moment you are in, you are taking away the opportunity to enjoy that moment. Regardless of the diversity of problems that you can encounter in your life, being mindful will help you to overcome any obstacles that are placed in your way and get beyond those problems which seem huge today. Letting your mind concentrate on the Noble Eightfold Path, you will find that the mindfulness that is derived from it is intentional. It also serves to strengthen your inner self.

Following on from the title of this chapter, Buddhism is awareness:

- Awareness of self
- Awareness of surroundings
- Awareness of others

Without this awareness, you lose on the karmic scale and this is explained in a future chapter. By being aware, you are able to empathize with others and encourage them. You are also able to control the way that you interact with the world and keep your negativity to a minimum. Whether you realize it or not, all unhappiness stems from inside you. Although you may see others to blame for any negative feelings that you have, it is, in fact, your own interpretation that dictates whether you are negatively impacted by what others do and Buddhism helps you to understand this impact and to minimize it. Buddhism is always the Middle Path.

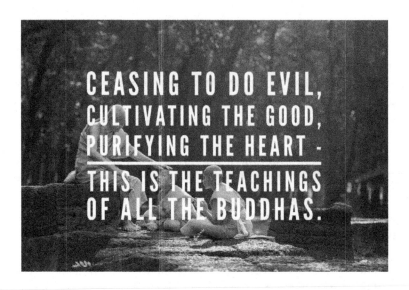

CHAPTER 2

THE TEACHINGS
OF BUDDHISM

"Ceasing to do evil, cultivating the good, purifying the heart
– this is the teachings of all the Buddhas."

— *The Buddha*

If you are here, then it must mean you want to know more about the teachings of Buddhism. Well, just remember that the ancient teachings of Buddhism are many. Nevertheless, they would not have been passed down through the generations if they had not served a purpose in the lives of their followers.

In this chapter, you are provided with an overview, of sorts, of the different teachings of Buddhism. It is a good idea to take a few steps back to get a bird's eye view of things before you turn to the minute details, after all. Rest assured you will soon find that these teachings are expounded in the succeeding chapters.

Perhaps one of the most interesting characteristics of the teachings of Buddhism is the absence of a superior being who governs the universe. This is because the Buddha did not focus on the worship of a supernatural entity, but rather on the path to discovering the Dharma, or the universal truth. This path is open to all beings on earth and thus you must understand that, under these circumstances, there can be no one person who should be worshipped above another. While it is perfectly acceptable to be inspired by others to attain a better understanding of Buddhist philosophy, the awe is not stretched to such a limit that you would be expected to worship or idolize.

To understand the Dharma, it is important to understand that becoming "awakened" is not unlike waking up from a deep sleep. However, instead of coming out of the suspended state of rest that is slumber, it is from a life that was once filled with suffering. While you may not see your day to day living as suffering, if you are indeed lacking in understanding of yourself and your place in life, then there will be an element of suffering within your life. Just as people in olden days suffered and were the reason for the search Siddhartha Gautama made while meditating under that tree, people today also suffer. Their reasons for suffering may have changed over the centuries, but the fundamental basis of Buddhism is to help people to find their way to understanding. Thus, no matter what century you are in, the teachings remain current and relevant.

For some, it's hard to understand a course of life following a dictation that is not associated with a supreme being. Many people are taught, through various different religions, as they grow, that their lives are not their own. The succession of living day to day on a predisposed path leaves a wide door open for discomfort, unhappiness, and excess. Buddhism is about finding that revelation of truth where all of the suffering of this life falls away and you are faced with the beautiful truth. That truth is the same today as it always was.

To understand the Dharma, you are encouraged to learn about the Buddhist doctrines. These are:

- The Four Noble Truths,
- The Noble Eightfold Path,
- The Chain of Causation,

- The Three Marks of Existence, and
- The Three Fires

The Four Noble Truths

If this is not your first time of looking into the teachings of Buddhism, then you may be familiar with the Four Noble Truths. They are regarded by Buddhists as the core teachings of the Buddha. They are:

- Desire or Suffering (Dukkha),
- Thirst or Craving (Samudaya),
- Cessation of Desire or Suffering (Niroda), and
- The Middle Path (Magga)

The Four Noble Truths have both reflected and pragmatic purposes in your life. Together, they serve as the key to awakening. You will find extensive details about the four truths in the next chapter.

The Noble Eightfold Path

The Eightfold Path of the Nobles altogether serves as one of the foundational teachings of Buddhism. It is the fourth of the Four Noble Truths, which is why you will find more about the Noble Eightfold Path in the chapter that follows.

Also called The Middle Path, it is perhaps the most popular teaching because it can be applied, observed, and experienced in everyday life. The eight steps in The Middle Path are as follows:

- Right View,
- Right Resolve,
- Right Speech,
- Right Conduct,
- Right Livelihood,
- Right Effort,
- Right Mindfulness, and
- Right *Samadhi* (or the state of intense concentration)

The Path emphasizes that self-restraint, self-discipline, and the practice of mindfulness and meditation can help put an end to suffering. Through these practices, one can discern the Truth and reach the state of enlightenment. Looking at how each one of these parts of the path relates to your life, it is fairly straightforward to try and prioritize your behavior toward yourself and others so that it is more in line with the teachings of Buddha and helps you to have a greater depth of understanding. For this purpose, in the early days of learning, it is not uncommon for students to keep a diary of their interactions and learn from them. If negative interactions happen, then learning to apply the Buddhist Noble Eight Fold Path to your life will allow you to come through such negative experiences unscathed and able to gain strength from them, rather than allowing them to weaken who you are.

The Chain of Causation

The Chain of Causation, also called "The Twelve Nidāna" (*nidāna* is a Sanskrit word which translates to "link, cause, or motivation") is a fundamental Buddhist teaching. It explains that all beings are interdependent and impermanent. The twelve links reveal the repetition of life itself, particularly the role of suffering, otherwise referred to by its Sanskrit word, *Dukkha*.

The twelve Nidāna are concisely explained as follows:

- Ignorance (Avijjā)
  - The lack of knowledge of suffering, of where it originated, how to end it, and how to live a life that leads towards ending it is ignorance. This link is connected to "Constructing Activities."
- Constructing Activities (Saṅkhāra)
  - This link refers to any form of physical, verbal, or mental action, be it good or bad, which causes an effect, called *karma,* on a being. Both willful action and planning are included. It directs to "Rebirth Consciousness."
- Rebirth Consciousness (Viññāna)
  - Consciousness as a link serves as the umbrella to six sub-classes, namely:
  - Eye-consciousness,

- o Ear-consciousness,
- o Nose-consciousness,
- o Tongue-consciousness,
- o Body-consciousness, and
- o Intellect-consciousness
- o One cannot be conscious without one's organs, specifically the sensory ones. This leads to the next link, "Name and Form."

- Name and Form (Nāmarūpa)
  - o The "Name," which also represents the mind or one's mentality, is composed of five elements: sensation, perception, intention, contact, and attention.
  - o The "Form" represents the body, and it is dependent on the four great elements: earth (which embodies solidity), water (which embodies cohesion), fire (which embodies heat), and air (which embodies motion).
  - o Altogether, Name and Form lead to the next link, which is the "Six-fold Sense Bases."

- Sixfold Sense Bases (Saḷāyatana)
  - o The eyes, nose, ears, tongue, body, and mind, are the means by which we come into the next link, "Contact."

- Contact (Phassa)
  - o This link represents the state in which the object, the sensory organ, and the consciousness all come into contact. It then directs one to the next link "Sensation."

- Sensation (Vedanā)
  - o There are six manifestations of sensation, and these are:
  - o Vision,
  - o Hearing,
  - o Olfactory sensation,
  - o Gustatory sensation,
  - o Tactile sensation, and
  - o Intellectual sensation
  - o After this link comes "Craving."

- Craving (Tanhā)

- Cravings are the effect of the six manifestations of sensation, namely in the form of visions, sounds, scents, flavors, touch, and thoughts. It transitions one to the next link, which is "Clinging Attachment."

- Clinging Attachment (Upādāna)
  - To resist separation from a craving is the essence of this link. Clinging itself is sub-divided into four categories: sensual, view, practice, and self-clinging. It then leads to the next link, which is "Becoming."

- Becoming (Bhava KammaBhava)
  - "Becoming" in this sense is from the Sanskrit *bhāva*, which means "emotion or state of mind or body." It refers to the continuity of rebirth, life, and maturation.

- Birth (Jāti)

  This link does not literally refer to the beginning of one's life (although this is also a part of it), but the attainment of a new state of being. When you change as an individual as caused by the previous ten links, you enter this one. After this, it leads to "All the Sufferings."

- All the Sufferings (Jarāmarana)

  This link represents the time when one undergoes and/or endures suffering. Failing to recognize the Dharma would then lead you back to the first link mentioned, "Ignorance."

As you can see, everything comes in a full circle. However, if you seek to understand the interconnectedness of these twelve links, you are better equipped to free yourself from suffering. The point of the matter is that certain phenomena only persist if you do not free yourself from the elements that sustain it. This can be seen quite clearly when you keep a journal of your experiences and are able to judge those that have served you well or those that have served you badly.

You may also note a connection here that is vital to your understanding of Buddhism. The senses are important and how you use them helps you to understand the word mindfulness which is a practice of being ever present in each moment that you live, being aware of everything that these senses are aware of and enjoying the changes that life puts forward by the use of disciplining the mind. When your mind is wandering to other places, you often forget about the senses. You eat your food too quickly. You walk through a park without noticing the flowers. You work in an automated fashion and are not aware of the very things that are encouraged in Buddhism in general. Take your time to eat and savor the food and the different textures of the food and you suffer less. Notice nature all around you and it lifts your spirits. Be present in the work that you do so that you are aware of every movement of the body and can enjoy the experience of working as being a positive thing, rather than a negative one.

The Three Marks of Existence

According to the Buddha, all living beings have three main features, also called Signs of Being or Dharma Seals. They are:

- Impermanence (Anicca)

  This mark explains that no conditioned things are permanent.

  Remember the old saying, "the only constant thing in life is change?" This is actually one of the most fundamental teachings of Buddhism.

  No events and beings, both physical and mental, are permanent; therefore, the concept of "lasting security" is a fallacy. The fact that all beings decay may sound depressing, but it is the truth.

  The opposite of Impermanence is Nirvana, in which there is no such thing as death, decay, or change.

- Desire or Suffering (Dukkha)

  This mark reveals that no conditioned things are satisfied.

  The constant desire or the lack of satisfaction is the root of all suffering. It manifests in both physical and mental forms, and it succeeds every rebirth (or change in one's life), aging, illness, and death.

  Suffering comes from not being able to acquire what is desired. It is also experienced when one is not able to keep away from what one wishes to avoid.

- Non-Self (Anatta)

  This mark teaches that all things, whether conditioned or not, are non-self.

This doctrine can be considered controversial by some because it explains that there is no everlasting essence in any phenomena or being. In other words, there is no "soul" or permanent self.

This might sound redundant to the first mark, but it actually covers a broader range than the latter. This is because it applies to all beings, both conditioned and unconditioned. Therefore, Nirvana is also described as a state of non-self.

According to this teaching, the expression "I am" is considered as conceited because it breeds *dukkha*. Thus, to free oneself from desire and suffering, one must let go of the idea of the "Self."

Now that you have learned about the three marks of existence, you can meditate on them. Enlightened beings have been able to end their suffering because of their insight into these teachings.

The Three Fires

The Three Fires also called the "Three Poisons," are the innate flaws found in all beings. It is the main reason for the existence of Craving, and it, therefore, contributes greatly to Desire and Suffering.

The Three Fires are explained further in Chapter 16. However, to help you establish a foundation of the concept, here are their names:

- Delusion or Confusion (Moha),
- Greed or Sensual Attachment (Raga), and
- Aversion or Ill Will (Dvesha)

Each of the Three Fires has a symbol in the form of an animal: the boar, which represents delusion or confusion, the rooster, which represents greed; and snake, which represents ill will.

As you continue to dig deeper into the histories and teachings of Buddhism, you will find insights that are even more complex. However, it is important to go back to these five fundamental teachings and to be reminded of them. This is because they can help draw you back to the Middle Path.

Now, before you proceed to the next Chapter (which is about the Four Noble Truths), keep close to your heart the value of both compassion and wisdom. These two virtues are most significant to Buddhists, followed by patience, loving kindness, generosity, and humanity.

As you are reading, attempt to turn off the world around you. Mute notifications, your cell phone, and your television and remember that you are right where you are supposed to be at this moment. Take in every ounce of knowledge and understanding from moment to moment as you would in any joyous occasion in life. The purpose of this book is to help you to understand Buddhism and to practice it in your life.

The heart of the teachings of Buddhism is harmlessness, or *ahimsa*, which instills the way of life that causes no harm to all beings. Keep this insight close to you, and strive to practice it each day. Doing so will help you achieve a genuinely meaningful life. If you are wondering how you can apply this to your life, look at what you do each day and work out at each instant of your life which way is the Buddhist way, rather than which way is the way that is the most acceptable by society. You need to understand that taking on these insights and making them part of your life will require discipline. It is not an easy road to follow, but it is one that will help you to alleviate your own suffering. This is something you will learn through your activities in life as you follow the Buddhist teachings. It may even help you to make notes so that you can carry the teachings with you until you are sufficiently aware of them and able to act upon them without thinking about it.

In fact, having a note of the Nobel Eight Fold Path helps to remind you in your life of the way that you need to be heading. It will do you no harm and in fact, will help you to learn to incorporate each one of the branches of the Nobel Eightfold path into your life.

Studying the Three Marks of Existence and the Three Fires in conjunction with your change of habits to introduce the Noble Eight Fold Path helps you to see how to adjust your attitude and your behavior in line with Buddhist doctrine.

Impermanence, for example, helps you to accept that life changes. If a relationship ends, you can more easily accept that it was good while it lasted and move on to new relationships rather than trying to cling to the perceived permanence of something that never was permanent. In society today, we are prone to want things to remain the same and feel safe in the perceived knowledge that they are, although the Buddhist philosophy clearly states that this is not the case.

The area of "not self" is also important to explore. We are all made up of different parts and cannot indeed be stereotyped as the society would have us believe. In the world we live in, we place great value on true self when the self is always changing and can never remain the same. When you are able to let go of these preconceptions and accept the impermanence of what and who you are, you open up the potential of understanding beyond the limits that you place upon yourself by living up to stereotypes of a society that pigeonholes people. Buddhist philosophy doesn't do that. Thus, there are no limitations.

Suffering – When you pay great attention to your suffering, you give it credence, rather than stepping away from it or trying to avoid it. The fact that people expect suffering gives suffering more power over whom they become. The lesson to be learned from suffering is not how to avoid it, but how it makes you more compassionate in your approach and builds you up rather than tearing you down. This helps you to be able to become more compassionate with others because you understand the nature of suffering, and know that all suffering comes to an end and that it can be positive in nature by helping your understanding and compassion levels.

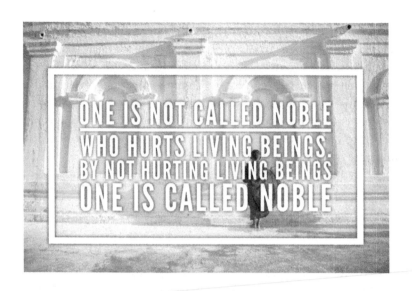

ONE IS NOT CALLED NOBLE
WHO HURTS LIVING BEINGS.
BY NOT HURTING LIVING BEINGS
ONE IS CALLED NOBLE

CHAPTER 3

THE FOUR NOBLE TRUTHS

"One is not called noble who hurts living beings.
By not hurting living beings one is called noble."

— The Buddha

The Four Noble Truths are understood and accepted by the Buddhas as the true reality. Buddhist teachings reveal that the Buddha began teaching the Four Noble Truths as soon as he had experienced enlightenment.

According to these truths, all beings crave and cling to things and states that are not permanent. This leads to suffering, which in turn ensnares the beings who are stuck in the never-ending cycle of rebirth, suffering, and dying.

However, a path leads beyond this cycle. It is through the Fourth Noble Truth: The Middle Path. The Buddhas encourage those who wish to be awakened from the cycle, not just to understand, but also experience The Middle Path.

To understand and practice the Middle Path, it is a prerequisite to first gain a deeper understanding of all Four Noble Truths. Emeritus Professor Geoffrey Samuels, who played a crucial role in bringing the teachings of Buddhism to the Western world, explained that the Four Noble Truths reveal what needs to be understood to begin the path that leads to enlightenment.

Here are the Four Noble Truths:

Desire or Suffering (Dukkha)

The First Noble Truth teaches that one's desires are impossible to satisfy, and this causes pain or suffering.

Some liken the Four Noble Truths to be analogous to traditional Indian medicine, with the First Noble Truth, being the diagnosis. In other words, it identifies and seeks to describe the disease in the form of Desire or Suffering. Some see this Noble Truth as a mere acknowledgement of the fact that people do suffer. If it's easier to understand in that way, by all means, adopt this stance while keeping your mind open to other interpretations.

Try the following exercise to consider how the First Noble Truth applies to your own life. Pause and reflect for a while on whether you have ever experienced feeling permanently satisfied. When you come to think of it, the concept of setting and attaining goals often leads to even more aspirations.

We as humans are in a constant cycle of yearning for a satisfying end to everything we do. However, this in itself is impossible to do since achieving one goal, object, relationship, etc., opens doors to the next want. In today's society of excess, it is even more difficult to find yourself satisfied. When we finally reach that financial goal for retirement, we strive to live other experiences that will satisfy us at the moment. Unfortunately, without realizing it, we spend our entire lives searching and wandering, attempting to fulfill a want that cannot be fulfilled. From the food we eat, the jobs we have, the money we make, and even the objects we desire, we are always searching for something we deem as "better."

Of course, while there is nothing negative about striving for your dreams, clinging too much to them leads to the constant feeling of yearning, which in itself is painful.

Since the world that we live in is ever-changing, we need to accept that we are constantly changing too, and sometimes that means moving from one set of emotions to another. We are rarely satisfied with anything because as soon as we derive satisfaction from anything, our mind shifts to the next thing. You will find that meditation and discipline of the mind in a positive way will help considerably to cut down the suffering, although the First Noble Truth has to be accepted. There is always suffering of one kind or another in the world. This Noble Truth merely confirms that fact and is often shortened to a very easily understandable format: Suffering exists.

Thirst or Craving (Samudaya)

The Second Noble Truth describes the main source of the Desire or Suffering, and it is one's "thirst" or craving for something in this world, which is impermanent. Your thirst or craving creates *karma*, which then causes a change in you that would only lead to a new desire. Thus, if you want this simply explained, it means that all suffering has a cause.

If you are comparing the Second Noble Truth with a medical diagnosis, you can describe it as the step where you attempt to determine the root cause of the disease or the etiology.

To understand how the Second Noble Truth unfolds in your life, try to recall the last time you experienced pain and then reflect on what exactly caused it. Buddhists accept that when there is a pain, there is always going to be a cause of that pain, no matter whether that is a physical or mental pain. There are always reasons for this pain to happen.

For instance, let us say you remember the feeling of being disappointed about a canceled trip that you had been looking forward to for months. The cause of your suffering is your desire towards the trip. That suffering, in itself, is a manifestation created by your mind depending on what you have taken in over the course of your life. Your disappointment or pain can come from any event in your life that has left you feeling that you were cheated of something.

From this disappointment, you are left with a further desire to correct it. You are then caught back in the cycle where disappointment will surely find you once again. We cling to the positive emotional responses we get, without realizing they are self-satisfaction created by our minds, not our self.

You might think it is just natural to experience this, and, indeed, you are right. This is why it is considered a reality. In a simple format, the Second Noble Truth is that all suffering has a cause.

Cessation of Desire or Suffering (Niroda)

The Third Noble Truth teaches that to end one's Thirst or Craving will lead to the end of Suffering. It is only through this that *karma* would no longer be created, and therefore one is awakened from the cycle.

Going back to the medical analogy concept, you could compare the Third Noble Truth with determining the cure for the disease, or the prognosis.

The concept by itself seems very straightforward and simple, but the practice of it is what appears to cause us to continue in this self-absorbed cycle. Though you may think that you are kind, generous, and always helping, it is important to realize that self-absorbed is not meant in a selfish standpoint, but in a way where your mind is creating these feelings to entice it to continue forward looking to satisfy your next urge.

So, what does it feel like to end one's Desire and, consequently, Suffering? Naturally, the only way to find out is to experience it yourself. However, the Buddhas often describe it as peace of mind in this life. It's a completeness that leaves no room for want, no space for pride and no disappointment from what does not happen because there are no expectations. Thus, the Third Noble Truth is that suffering ends.

The Middle Path (Magga)

The Fourth Noble Truth explains that the only way to achieve enlightenment is through the discernment and practice of the Noble Eightfold Path or the Middle Path. The symbol of the Middle Path is the dharma wheel (dharma chakra), which has eight spokes that represent each of its elements.

If you go back to compare it with the medical diagnosis, the Fourth Noble Truth represents the part where the physician prescribes the right treatment for the disease that can help you cure it.

Buddhist teachers usually divide the Noble Eightfold Path into three core divisions: Wisdom, Moral virtue, and Meditation. Below is a comprehensive list of how each component of the Noble Eightfold Path fits into each category. You will also gain a deeper understanding of what each of them means:

Wisdom

The first division, Wisdom, is composed of the first two of the Noble Eightfold Path: the Right View and the Right Resolve. By understanding and practicing these two, you will attain the wisdom necessary to attain enlightenment.

1. **Right View**

   The Right View has to do with how you should perceive *karma* and *rebirth*. It also encompasses how you should value the Four Noble Truths in mind, body, and words. It incites rebirth and affects the different stages that are being passed through in the cycle of life.

   The purpose of the Right View is to make your path clear from muddled thoughts and misunderstandings. Once you have appropriately understood the truths, then you have the Right View. You will likely work with meditation to help you to understand this Right View which will be explained later in the book.

   In Buddhism, it is believed that when your body dies, your true self-travels through what is known as the Bardo. The Bardo is a place in each life where you go to choose your next body. It is believed that the closer you are to correct awakening in this life, the clearer your choice will be in the Bardo. If your mind is clouded when you pass, your true self will be lost, making your choice for rebirth often difficult.

   Gil Fronsdal, an American Buddhist teacher, explained that Right View could be likened to a concept in Cognitive Psychology. He explains that Right View is how your mind perceives the world, and how this perception affects one's thoughts and actions.

2. **Right Resolve**

Otherwise referred to as "Right Intention" or "Right Thought," this is where the Buddhist becomes firm with his purpose to renounce living life in a mundane world in favor of a spiritual pilgrimage.

You can take the literal meaning of this and apply it to everything you do from day to day. Having the right intention of actions in every part of your life will help you come closer to that eternal truth. This is an excellent tactic to remember when you leave the sanctity of your home and you are faced with the magnitude of excess in the world around you. Stop and think before making any choices and apply the genuine and right intention to your actions. That right intention is not just about you. It is about the circumstances and everything that is involved in the decisions that you make as well as the consequences.

Moral Virtue

The second division is composed of the third to fifth folds: Right Speech, Right Conduct, and Right Livelihood. Moral Virtue is described by most Buddhist teachers as having the discipline and merit that will lead to karmic, contemplative, social, and psychological congruency. All these are necessary to be able to engage in the final division, Meditation.

Our bodies work in different sectors, and it is important that you are in alignment with not just your mind and body but with the world around you. Remember that with rebirth comes the opportunity to be reborn as any living creature on our planet. Therefore, it should be understood that you are connected to everything natural around you. Just as the roots of the trees unseen underground connect with the soil of the earth, so does your internal self, which is nurtured and lead by the universe.

3. **Right Speech**

Most Buddhist teachings describe Right Speech as the abstinence of lying, divisive speech, abusive speech, and idle chatter.

To abstain from lying means to avoid speaking anything but the truth, and to hold on to the truth so as to be firm and reliable.

To abstain from divisive speech means to speak only words that contribute to the harmony of things in general. The Buddhist way is to add to the joy experienced by others which cannot be achieved should divisive speech be employed.

To abstain from abusive speech means to use only polite and affectionate words that are pleasing to other beings. Even in dealings with difficult people, we are encouraged to use only positive speech that helps to restore some kind of harmony to whatever the given situation.

To abstain from idle chatter is to use only words that would bring you closer to Enlightenment. You cannot allow idle chatter to stand in the way of the route of your life. Think of speech as stepping stones through life and if you employ idle chatter that is negative, you can think that this is taking you away from the next pebble on your path and back to the confusion of the stream upon which the pebbles are placed.

According to the Buddha, Right Speech is to speak only what is useful and true, depending on the situation and where such words are appropriate. Otherwise, it would be better to say nothing at all. Silent observation is something that human beings find very hard, though, with practice you will find that it serves more purpose than negative approach and increases your level of understanding.

It is often hard to realize that just because you are dedicated to speaking the truth, doesn't mean that your words should be hurtful to others. Empathy, again, is one of the most important characteristics of someone leading a Buddhist path. Words can be constructive and truthful without being hurtful. It is a delicate balance between each other that we must find. You may wonder if you are justified in being negative toward another person based on what they have said to you. However, it's important to see the positive side of things and refrain from using any language aimed at someone with the intention of hurting that person.

4. **Right Conduct**

Also called "Right Action," this part of the Eightfold Path is also described in a similar way as Right Speech. Instead of words, however, it is in the form of physical activity. According to

Buddhist teachings, Right Conduct is the abstinence of killing, stealing, and sexual misconduct.

To abstain from killing, one must not take part in the harming and taking away of the life of all sentient beings, whether human or animal.

To abstain from stealing means to avoid taking away anything that is not voluntarily given or offered to you by the being who owns the property. This encompasses all forms of stealing, such as those taken forcibly, stealthily, or through deceit. This is a lesson what one usually learns as a child, although society sometimes blind sights us by making certain practices acceptable, even though they are still deceitful. Thus, Buddhist philosophy covers all areas of deceit, not just those you choose to acknowledge.

To abstain from sexual misconduct refers to becoming sexually involved with anyone who is under the protection of a guardian, of siblings, of parents, of a spouse, of a betrothed, and of anyone who is not married.

Because Buddhism is the path to personal enlightenment, and the separation of those things around you that are put there out of cultural inertia, marriage is not something that is really spoken about. Many Buddhists are married and have children, even some of the most devout yogis, but their relationship is one of truth, eternally. It is often found that those that are married either do so before enlightenment becomes their understanding or after but for more spiritual purposes than current day marriages.

5. **Right Livelihood**

The Right Livelihood is when you uphold your virtue and to avoid being the cause of suffering of sentient beings. Most Buddhist teachings explain that one should not become involved in the trading of human beings, meat, animals for slaughter, alcoholic drinks, poison, or weapons.

In today's workplace, you may wonder how you can do your job without being in one of these trades, but as long as you are in employment that harms no one and tries to have a job that actually helps mankind in some small way, then you will have begun to understand the message given on this path of the Noble Eightfold Path.

It is believed that anything that is harmful to your physical body also creates a stronger barrier between your mind and yourself. As the barrier becomes thicker, it becomes more difficult to reach that state of enlightenment. The mind is almost like a trick; it doesn't want you to give it up, so things like addiction and culturally learned behavior could be tough to upend. By creating a healthy body without outside negative influence, you are helping your body release the connection with the piece of meat on top of your head, letting yourself take over your consciousness.

Meditation

Another word for meditation is *Samadhi,* and it is the final division of the Noble Eightfold Path. The whole concept centers in the conditioning of one's mind in order to install discernment into the Three Marks of Existence, let go of unhelpful states and reach Enlightenment. Full knowledge and dedication to practicing the final three of the Noble Eightfold Path – Right Effort, Right Mindfulness, and Right *Samadhi* – will lead to the fulfillment of these.

6. **Right Effort**

Buddhist teachings describe Right Effort as your strength of will and mind as you choose to do good each day. It has the self-discipline to choose to think, feel, speak, and do what is good, even when it is challenging at times.

According to most Buddhist teachers, it requires more Right Effort to abstain from ill will and sensual desires. Ill-will includes anger, resentment, and hatred towards all other beings, while sensual desires are all immoral desires experienced through the five senses.

Though certain sexual situations, especially those in a negative light, are considered to be ill-will, sex itself is not discussed much in Buddhism. Your body is your temple, the avenue in which your true self is able to work through to attempt to reach enlightenment. Anything negative should be abstained from.

You may find this hard at first since your mind is accustomed to being distracted. However, when you learn to meditate and can put the right amount of concentration into what you are doing, you will have fulfilled this requirement. The problem that you may find is that you are unable to let go of thoughts which are not relevant to the meditation process. However, everyone is guilty of this when they first try to meditate. If you can simply work your way through dismissing thoughts that are irrelevant, you will be able to increase your effort.

Do not be harsh on yourself for this failing. It takes a while to be able to meditate. Do not expect more from yourself than you are currently capable of doing. As long as you are making the effort, you are working toward understanding what meditation is all about.

7. Right Mindfulness

This part of the Noble Eightfold Path is described as the state in which you become aware and mindful of the present moment. When being mindful of your body, you acknowledge and accept it for what it is. The same goes for one's emotions and thoughts. As you become aware of and acknowledge these states, you let go of worldly desires and all suffering attached to them.

One of the things that many Buddhists practice on a regular basis is extreme mindfulness of thought. When you are stricken with an emotion, especially the negative ones, you want to step back and take a pause. Realize that that emotion is created by your conscious mind and is dependent upon your cultural understanding of the world around you. Then, once you understand the emotion you are feeling, gently remind yourself that it is not the truth. In a simple way to explain it, it does not come from your true self, and therefore it is not real.

Right mindfulness also covers being able to let go of those things that are of the past or perhaps worries that relate to the future. Mindfulness is indeed in this moment. If you look back in this book, you will be reminded of the quotation by the Dalai Lama where he explained mindfulness very eloquently. Mindful people are ever present and it is hard to reach enlightenment unless you have that presence and understand its significance.

8. **Right *Samadhi*** (or the state of intense concentration)

The final step in the Noble Eightfold Path, Right Samadhi is about detaching yourself from desires related to the senses and from unwholesome states.

Then, you enter the first level of concentration called the first *jhana*. On this level, you maintain applied and sustained thinking, which will lead you to experience happiness gained from these detachments as you continue to concentrate.

You will find that your conscious mind is fighting to stay in control. Thoughts and ideas will enter your mind during this stage of meditation. There are several techniques used to clear those thoughts, including mindfulness, which is an understanding of your conscious mind and pushing them out, and breathing techniques. Visualization can play a key role in calming your conscious mind so that you may move on in your meditation.

As you continue to go deeper into the second level of concentration, you experience "oneness of mind" and inner stillness. On this level, you no longer maintain applied and sustained thinking because you only experience pure joy from the state of concentration itself.

As in all other states, this feeling of pure joy eventually fades. This then transitions to the third level of concentration, wherein you become fully aware and in control of your faculties.

The fourth and final level of intense concentration takes place after you have given up your desire and suffering and after emotions such as pure joy or sadness fade away. On this level, only pure and steady mindfulness is experienced.

Many Buddhist scholars advise that those who wish to follow the Noble Eightfold Path should apply all of the divisions simultaneously, instead of in a linear manner. Each of the eight factors is of equal importance and is, in fact, interdependent. However, some scholars believe that the final factor – Right Samadhi – can only be reached if the ones before it have been sufficiently developed.

It is important to listen to your inner self and understand what is working and what is not. The path to enlightenment is not an exact science, it is a path that every person takes and each one, though similarities occur, is created uniquely to your own true self. The difference is that some students of Buddhism who are in their first stages of learning may believe that interpretation is more important than being, whereas the reverse is the truth. It is when you are able to drop the interpretation and simply enjoy the being that you are able to find answers to all of the questions that life poses.

Now that you have reached the end of this chapter, how do you feel about the Four Noble Truths and the Noble Eightfold Path? Do you agree with their teachings?

If you do, then you can embrace the knowledge you have just gained so that you can apply them in your everyday life. The best way to start that is to list them simply so that you are reminded of them in your day to day life. Don't overthink them. Just live your life in a way that respects the Noble Eight Fold Path. When you are able to do that, you will find that your happiness quota improves because of the discipline that you have been able to apply to your life. When Siddhartha Gautama came up with the Eight Fold Path and it was written for Buddhist followers to live by, it was not in the form of a punishment. It was so that suffering became less prevalent in the lives of people. It works because the improvements that you make to your life are such that they are life-enhancing. Even concentrating for a short time each day on your new approach to life will make life easier for you.

If you do not agree with the teachings, then perhaps you can find the answers to your questions in the succeeding chapters. The next chapter, in particular, tells of the different schools of Buddhism which may help you to decide the route to your own beliefs.

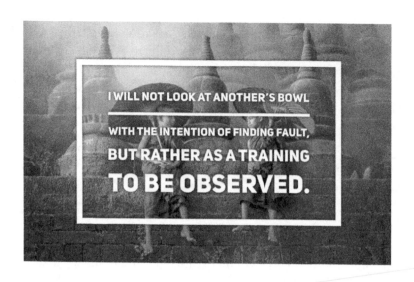

I WILL NOT LOOK AT ANOTHER'S BOWL

WITH THE INTENTION OF FINDING FAULT,

BUT RATHER AS A TRAINING

TO BE OBSERVED.

CHAPTER 4

THE DIFFERENT SCHOOLS OF BUDDHISM

"I will not look at another's bowl with the intention of finding fault, but rather as a training to be observed."

– The Buddha

Buddhism is over two thousand five hundred years old, so it comes as to no surprise that it branches into several institutional and doctrinal divisions. However, the most widely accepted way of classifying these schools are the three doctrinal schools, namely: "The Ancient Teachings" (Theravāda), "The Great Vehicle" (Mahāyāna), "The Diamond Way" (Vajrayāna), and Zen Buddhism.

"The Ancient Teachings" (Theravāda)

The Pali term *theravāda* means "school of the elder monks," and its history can be traced back to one of the most ancient Buddhist schools called Sthāvirīya. It has been around since the 4th century, approximately a thousand years after the First Buddha passed away. Theravada Buddhism was one of eighteen to twenty-five schools of teaching in this time period but is the only one to have survived. It is the doctrinal school of Buddhism that follows the Pāli Canon. This compendium of the most ancient recorded Buddhist texts serves as the core of Buddhist teaching, practices, and traditions.

Theravāda began in Southeast Asia and South Asia, specifically in the countries of Cambodia, Laos, Thailand, Sri Lanka, and Myanmar. It is also practiced in China, Bangladesh, Malaysia, Vietnam, and Nepal, although only by minority groups.

The core teaching of Theravāda is the "teaching of analysis," which explains that discernment should come from the practitioner's own experiences, critical reasoning, and practical application of knowledge. However, this does not mean that the advice of the wise should not be taken into consideration throughout one's spiritual pilgrimage. Rather, both the discernment of one's experiences and the teachings of the wise should be considered.

Today, Theravada Buddhism can be found all over the world, and in over 100 countries. It has been estimated that across the world, there are at least 100 million followers of this sector of Buddhism. The popularity of this type of Buddhism not only comes from the fact that it is one of the oldest forms but from the path in which you follow.

The Theravāda Path begins with "Learning," then "Practice," and finally, "Attainment."

Learning

The understanding of "The Three Marks of Existence" is the foundation of the Pali Canon, the standard collection of traditional Theravadan Buddhist scriptures. It is then followed by discernment of "The Four Noble Truths."

Apart from these, the concept of Defilements (kilesas) is explained as well in Theravāda. These defilements can be interpreted as "toxic mental states" that keep an aspiring Buddhist from being able to practice Samadhi (intense concentration). While these Defilements are temporary in that they wax and wane. Theravadins explain that they are still harmful to not just the self but others as well.

According to Theravāda teachings, there are five Defilements called the "Five Hindrances." Each of them can be described based on three levels: coarse, medium, and subtle. The "Five Hindrances" are:

1. Sensory Desire (kāmacchanda)

   This is the thirst or craving that involves the five senses: sight, hearing, taste, smell, and touch. You can easily relate to sensory desire in everyday life, from what you want to eat that suppresses your sense of taste, listening to negative commentary or music, and even causing self-injury for pleasure purposes. This is not demanding you dull all senses but that you use them in a positive manner with smart reasoning and empathetic consequences.

2. Ill-will (vyāpāda)

   Any negative thought that pertains to feelings of hostility, hatred, resentment, and bitterness fall under this Hindrance. This will always get in the way of enlightenment and will cause suffering to the self and to others.

3. Sloth-torpor (thīna-middha)

   A dull mind and a lazy body hinder one from being able to concentrate deeply and, worse, lead one to depression and lethargy. In today's world, it is very easy to allow yourself to fall into this category, but the route out of this hindrance is a clear one that is available to everyone who seeks it.

4. Restlessness-worry (uddhacca-kukkucca)

   Thoughts and feelings that cause worry and anxiety hinder the mind from achieving the state of calm that comes naturally with meditation. People who worry in this manner will suffer as a consequence and may even impose this suffering on those around them.

5. Doubt (vicikicchā)

   One's lack of trust keeps one from attaining *Samadhi*.

According to Theravāda, it is important to be deliberate in overcoming the Five Hindrances in order to enter the state of intense concentration. Theravadins further emphasize that ignorance (avijjā) is the root cause for a person to develop the Five Hindrances into habits. Therefore, awareness and understanding of the Five Hindrances is the first step towards overcoming them.

Another key teaching in Theravāda is the concept of Cause and Effect (Pratītyasamutpāda). The Pali Canon draws a line between two types of Causes: root (hetu) and facilitating (pacca). Once these two intertwine, the Effect comes to play. It is understood that the Cause should be taken away in order for the Effect to disappear. Yet somehow, aspiring Buddhists need a gentle reminder every now and then of this Truth.

Practice

Theravāda prescribes putting into practice the Seven Stages of Purification (Visuddhimagga) in order to free oneself from Suffering and ultimately attain Enlightenment. The Seven Stages of Purification are:

1. Purification of Conduct
2. Purification of Mind
3. Purification of View
4. Purification of Overcoming Doubt
5. Purification by Knowledge and Vision of What is Path and Not Path
6. Purification by Knowledge and Vision of the Course of Practice
   - Knowledge of contemplation of rise and fall
   - Knowledge of Contemplation of Dissolution
   - Knowledge of Appearance as Terror
   - Knowledge of Contemplation of Danger
   - Knowledge of Contemplation of Dispassion
   - Knowledge of Desire for Deliverance
   - Knowledge of Contemplation of Reflection
   - Knowledge of Equanimity about Formations
   - Conformity Knowledge
7. Purification Knowledge and Vision
   - Change of Lineage
   - Stream-winner (Sotāpanna)
   - Once-Returner (Sakadagami)
   - Non-Returner (Anāgāmi)

- One Who is Worthy (Arahants)

Meditation is the key to attaining Enlightenment in the Practice of Theravāda, and it is understood as the positive means of strengthening the mind. Meditation is divided into two categories, namely: samatha and vipassanā.

Samatha is to make oneself "adept," "calm," or to "visualize" and "achieve." This type of meditation is therefore meant to improve one's ability to concentrate. Only after you have perfected Samatha would you then be able to do Vipassanāmeditation.

This is because Vipassanā means "abstract understanding" or "insight." With this type of meditation, the mind is able to overcome ignorance and understand the nature of reality.

According to Theravāda Buddhism, you must permanently remove Defilements in order to achieve Enlightenment. The practice of mindfulness helps keep Defilements under control, but they can only be removed through constant and consistent introspection so that one would be able to identify their Causes. This needs to be applied to every Defilement repeatedly until the aspiring Buddhist is able to uproot them all.

Attainment

Theravadins believe that there are four levels of wisdom that through constant Practice, one can attain the two types of wisdom necessary to become enlightened. These are the "mundane" and the "supramundane."

You would attain "mundane" wisdom once you have discerned each of the Three Marks of Existence. As you gain further insight into each of them, you develop insight that will lead you to attain "supramundane" wisdom.

Now, "supramundane" wisdom has four levels, which are classified under the Seventh Stage of Purification (Purification of Knowledge and Vision). These are:

1. Stream-winner (Sotāpanna)

   The "Stream-winner" or "Stream enterer" is the one who has attained "mundane" wisdom by uprooting the first three fetters. These are the false Self-view, Skeptical Doubt, and the Clinging to Rites and Rituals.

- Self-view is the false view that what is compounded is permanent. This promotes the being to be possessive of the Self (characterized by the use of "mine," "me," or "I"), keeping one from attaining Enlightenment.

- Skeptical Doubt is the lack of trust in the Buddha, his teachings, and his community. This holds the being back from being able to gain insight through experience.

- Clinging to Rites and Rituals is the false belief that one becomes pure merely by performing rituals (including chanting and making offerings and sacrifices) or relying on a deity for non-causal delivery.

2. Once-Returner (Sakadagami)

The "Stream-winner" becomes a "Once-Returner" after he has uprooted the first three fetters and at the same time has reduced the fetters of hatred and lust.

3. Non-Returner (Anāgāmi)

The "Non-Returner" is the one who has permanently uprooted the five lower fetters that chain beings to the mundane world, particularly one experienced by the senses.

4. One Who is Worthy (Arahants)

You become the "One Who is Worthy" or the "Aharants" once you have attained Enlightenment. This means you have freed yourself from all Defilement, which brings an end to your ignorance, desire, and clinging.

"The Great Vehicle" (Mahāyāna)

Mahāyāna Buddhism is the most widespread of the three schools in the modern-day world. Mahāyāna may have originated from India. Then, it spread to Southeast, South, and East Asia, particularly in Bhutan, Bangladesh, Taiwan, China, Nepal, Korea, Japan, Mongolia, Indonesia, Vietnam, Singapore, and Malaysia.

Mahāyāna Buddhism is described as the path of the aspirant to follow in order to attain Perfect Enlightenment. This is why it is called the "Great Vehicle" towards enlightenment.

The Parable of the Burning House

A famous Mahayanist parable tells of how there are three vehicles (yana) that serve to classify the Sutrayana Schools of Buddhism. It is the Parable of the Burning House, and legend has it that the First Buddha himself told it to his disciple Shariputra.

This is how the Buddha told the story:

> "Shariputra, let us say there is a particular town in a particular place where there was a wealthy man. Our story began when he was already quite old, but his fortune was so vast it can no longer be counted. He was the proprietor of wide fields and many mansions, and he had a great number of servants.

> The mansion in which he lived was so huge, yet one can enter and leave it through a single gate. A large number of people, probably five hundred of them, lived in this mansion. However, the mansion was old, its rooms disintegrating, its pillars decaying, its walls dilapidating, and its roof unstable and crumbling.

> It was not long before a fire broke out, and it quickly devoured one room after another. The sons of the wealthy man, perhaps twenty or thirty, were still inside the house, unaware of the sprawling catastrophe.

> *As soon as the wealthy man saw the fire, he immediately became fearful and thought, I should be able to escape through the gate, but my sons are unknowingly trapped inside and still having a good time. The fire must be getting close to them, and soon they will experience much pain and suffering. Yet it might be too late for them to escape because their minds are not prepared to cope with such an emergency.*

> *I am strong, the wealthy man continued, I can cover them with a robe and put them all on a bench so that I can lift them all up and take them all out of the house to safety.*

> *But then again, he continued to think, there is only one gate to this house, and it is neither wide nor large enough to pass through. My sons are still youthful, and they do not understand how dangerous the fire is.*

> *They are so fond of playing their games that they may be too absorbed in them. Surely, the fire will burn them because of this. I should tell them my*

reasons for being so fearful. The fire is eating up the house now, so I should quickly get them and save them from it!

After these thoughts, the wealthy man immediately went into the house and began to shout for his sons: "You must immediately come out!" Despite that, his sons were still too engrossed with their games and not interested in listening to his words. The sons did not feel the fear and alarm that their father was experiencing, therefore, they did not care to get out of the house.

What is worse, they neither understood well what a fire was and how dangerous it is, nor how it was now eating up their house. Instead, they went on playing and simply glanced at their father without following his advice.

At this point, the wealthy man began to think; the house is now being eaten up by the flames. My sons and I will surely be burned if we do not escape from this house right away. What I should do now is create a practical way to help my sons escape the dangers of this burning house.

The wealthy man knew his sons well enough to know the specific toys each of them love to play with, and at the same time, what captures their individual interests. Hence, what he did was he called out, "Your favorite toys are rare and difficult to find. If you do not bring them with you right now, you will definitely regret it.

Right now, I have your goat carts, deer carts, and ox carts right outside the gate and are ready to be played with. You need to get out of the burning house right away and play with them. Whichever toy each of you wants, I will then give it!

As soon as the sons heard these words from their father about this opportunity, each of them felt motivated deep within their heart to run as fast as they could out of the burning house.

As soon as the sons passed through the gate, the wealthy man then gave each of them a large jewel-encrusted carriage drawn by a snow-white ox."

After the Buddha finished his story, he then asked his listening disciple if the wealthy man was guilty of lying to his sons. Shariputra's answer was this:

41

"No, he was not, World-Honored One. The wealthy man merely took the steps necessary to spare his sons from being burned and killed in the house. He is not guilty of lying. The reason why I am saying this is that the sons had still received a toy of some sort. Even more important was that his practical thinking was able to help him save them from the flames."

After hearing this response, the Buddha then said that he is like the father, who is the "father of the world," and the sons are like the humans who are born into the old and decaying burning house, threefold world.

"Shariputra, the wealthy man initially lured his sons out of the burning house using the three different types of carriages. However, after that, he gave them the large bejeweled carriage, which is not only the most comfortable but also the safest type of carriage ever to be made. In spite of this, the wealthy man was not guilty of lying. The Buddha does the same thing, and he is not lying.

He begins by teaching the three vehicles to draw the attention of and direct living beings, but after that, he makes use of the Great Vehicle to save them all. Why? It is because the Buddha has immeasurable power, wisdom, fearlessness, and the place in which the Dharma is kept. He has the capacity to provide to all living beings the Dharma of the Great Vehicle. Yet not all living beings have the capacity to receive it.

Shariputra, it is for this reason that you must understand why the Buddhas resort to practical means. By doing so, they then create these differences in the one Buddha vehicle and teach it as three."

Aside from the Parable of the Burning House, much of the teachings of Mahāyāna Buddhism are a loose compilation of the various teachings that can exist at the same time. Overall, the foundation of these teachings is based on the tenet that universal liberation from suffering can possibly be achieved by all beings.

Another is that everyone is capable of attaining Enlightenment within a single lifetime, but only if one devotes himself to the practice of mindfulness of the Buddha, the mantras, and ritual speech, and the understanding of the Mahāyāna sutras. Majority of Mahāyāna practitioners believe in preternatural bodhisattvas – Buddhists who are worthy of nirvana but postpone it to teach others.

Bodhisattva

The Bodhisattva plays the central role in traditional Mahāyāna Buddhism. According to the Mahayanists, it is too narrow to aspire to be free from suffering and to achieve Enlightenment. The main reason for this is that it does not inspire one to participate in helping other sentient beings become free from suffering.

The ones who are inspired and take the necessary steps to doing so are called the bodhisattva. While they are capable of attaining nirvana, they value the importance of guiding others towards the path of finding nirvana, instead of dedicating their lives to reaching it themselves.

The Bodhisattvas are known for having the intention to attain the Trikaya or becoming infinitely wise Buddha, as soon as they could. That way, they can become of better use to all other sentient beings. To become a high-level Bodhisattva, one must strive to cultivate an immensely compassionate mind and to possess *prajñā*, transcendent wisdom, to acknowledge the truths of Emptiness (Śūnyatā) and Dependent Origination (Pratītyasamutpāda).

Mahayanists also believe in the existence of many Buddhas and bodhisattvas who live in different realms. The Mahayana Buddha is described as one who is supernatural and omnipotent.

The Buddha Principle

In general, the Buddha Principle in Mahāyāna Buddhism refers to "a holy nature that is the fundament for sentient beings to become Buddhas." Some Mayanists believe that there is no such being that does not have a hidden, but indestructible, link to become enlightened. They also believe that this link is buried deep within every sentient being, and which consists of the "essence of the self" and deathlessness.

It is important to note that Mahayanists cannot be clustered under one Buddhist school of thought. Rather, Mahāyāna is more of an umbrella under which a vast number of schools can be found. The generally accepted ideal, however, is the role of the Bodhisattva.

"Zen Buddhism" (A School of Mahayana)

Zen Buddhism comes from Mahayana and is believed to be the simplest form of Buddhism on record. It dates back to the first Buddha and his practices as he sat under the Bodhi tree. Zen Buddhism was first created in China, originally known as Chan Buddhism, but was brought to Japan and then spread all over the world. There are two separate schools of Zen Buddhism, Soto Zen, and Rinzai Zen. Though they both have similar inherent qualities, their focus and practice are slightly different.

As with any other religion, this school of thought blossomed from the very first experience of enlightenment. Different cultures throughout time have adapted or created their own personal line of Buddhism. Zen Buddhism is no different in this accord and follows the simplest teachings of the first Buddha. As with Shiva, it is believed that satisfaction and the void of suffering in this life can only ultimately come when you have reached a state of full enlightenment. There is no amount of worldly goods that can satisfy your hunger for satisfaction. Within the two schools of Zen Buddhism, the major difference is how it is perceived that you are able to reach enlightenment.

Soto Zen

Soto Zen originated in China, known as Caodong Buddhism, but was brought to Japan by Dogen Kigen in the 1200's. Kigen initially studied a concept known as Tendai which relates back to the original enlightenment. This school of thought states that every being is inherently enlightened. This idea frustrated Kigen, bringing confusion as to why they spend so much time going through different ceremonial practices to reach enlightenment if it was believed everyone was already there.

In search of answers, Kigen traveled to China and began studying under Mater Riujing of the Caodong Temple where he found that under Soto Zen, there is no search for enlightenment. It is simply sitting quietly in meditation. This news was a relief to Kigen, and he stayed and studied for several years until eventually realizing full enlightenment. He then traveled back to Japan to spread the word of what became known as Soto Zen. Kigen became the founder of the main temple of Soto Zen in Japan, Eihei-Ji.

Soto Zen Buddhism focuses most of its attention on the practice of Zazen which is sitting meditation. The Soto practitioners believe that enlightenment is there already and they concentrate on the here and now, relishing in each and every moment of life. It is believed that through this practice you are bringing your true self back to its roots ultimately leading to full enlightenment. Though the center of Soto Zen is Zazen, practitioners still believe in the use of Koans to find a deeper understanding of self. A Koan is a spontaneous question or statement given by the teacher to his students that force them to think clearly and comprehensively. However, Koans in the Soto Zen practice are more whimsical and less rigid in thought.

Rinzai Zen

In 1168 and 1186 Myosan Elsai visited Mount Tiantai to learn authentic Chen Buddhism. He spent many years, focusing primarily on the Linji Sect of Chan, also known as Rinzai Zen Buddhism. Elsai became the first Japanese teacher of Rinzai Buddhism. When he came back to Japan, he brought the Rinzai teachings as well as the beginning of the tradition of tea drinking. He continued his lessons and eventually opened the first Zen Temple in Japan.

Rinzai is not the same as Soto in that while Soto focuses on meditation and sitting to reach that perfect state of enlightenment, Rinzai concentrates on the Zoan. These unique and random sayings from a teacher to a student are meant to spark the inner self into realization which in turn brings them to a true place of enlightenment. Koans are sometimes studied for years by a student who takes momentary intervals through the time period to stop and react to the Koan to their teacher. These Koans are there to find your inner truth, and for some, it only ever takes one.

Zen Buddhist Beliefs

As a member of the human race, we have a tendency to feel that the more answers we have, the greater we are. Religions subscribe to the idea that we know what is beyond this life here on earth. However, Zen Buddhism doesn't believe that the answers make you wise. Instead, they believe that as humans we are not capable of knowing or understanding what lies beyond this life. They do not believe that there is nothing, just that focusing on something that cannot be known is a waste of life, and a feeding of a man's ego. Zen practitioners focus solely on the here and now, expanding their truth and understanding of self not of the world beyond this human body. There is no dogma or religious pact a Zen Buddhist is forced to believe, and like all of Buddhism, there are no Gods. Buddha is a truly enlightened being that can give advice and understanding that will help you find your truth of self.

These theories can be hard to grasp at times because we are a curious species that likes the answers. We also thrive on the comfort that faith and religion give us. It is easier for a man's ego to rest confidently knowing they will be rewarded in death than to focus on now and not worry about what comes next. However, Zen Buddhists are not looking to feed their minds; they are seeking to feed their truth and self.

"The Diamond Way" (Vajrayāna)

If you have ever heard of Tibetan Buddhism, then you should know that it is traditionally called Vajrayāna. This Pali word literally translates to "the Diamond Way" or "the Thunderbolt Way."

According to ancient texts, Vajrayānais also used as a reference to one of the three vehicles mentioned in the Parable of the Burning House, of which the other two are the Theravāda and Mahāyāna. These ancient texts pertaining to Vajrayāna were found between the 3rd and 12th centuries in India, but the word itself was founded in 8th-century texts.

Similar to Mahāyāna in terms of its goal, the Vajrayāna tradition is to seek the status of a Bodhisattva. This goes to show that they are both distinct from Theravāda, which as you know has the goal of attaining enlightenment without intending to come back or even become a Buddha.

Vajrayāna practice follows the same path as with the Mahayana, which is the Buddha Principle. However, what makes them distinctive is their ritual, particularly the *phowa*, or the Vajrayāna Tibetan death ritual.

The Phowa is a meditation practice that illustrates "the practice of conscious dying." This ritual is performed at a Buddhist's moment of death, and Vajrayāna Buddhists believe that by doing so, it will transfer the Buddhist's consciousness out through the top of their head and then it will rise into the Pure Land or the celestial realm where the Bodhisattva reside. Performing the Phowa enables the Buddhist to avoid the usual experiences that naturally take place after one dies.

Aside from the rituals, Vajrayāna Buddhists also perform tantric techniques so as to experience ultimate Truth. These techniques range from basic to advanced, such as the Mahamudra. The word *Mahamudra* means "great symbol" and an advanced practitioner of Vajrayāna Buddhism can perform this technique to experience reality through tranquility and special insight.

Tantra Techniques

A variety of ancient Tantra texts can be distinguished in a number of ways. First is the Fourfold division, which was conceptualized by the *Sarma*, or the New Translation schools of Vajrayāna. According to them, Buddhist religious literature has four categories, namely:

- Action Tantra (Kriyayoga), which focuses on the importance of ritual,
- Performance Tantra (Charyayoga), which focuses on the importance of meditation,
- Yoga Tantra (Yogatantra), and
- Highest Yoga Tantra (Annuttarayogatantra), which has three sub-divisions: "mother," "father," and "non-dual."

Another type of division is utilized by the *Nyingma* or the Ancient Translation school. This consists of the Outer Tantras, with the Annuttarayogatantra divided into Three Inner Tantras.

The Three Outer Tantras are:

- Kriyayoga,
- Charyayoga or Upayoga, and
- Yogatantra

The Three Inner Tantras are:

- Mahayoga,
- Anuyoga, and
- Atiyoga

All these Tantra techniques are complex in nature, but not impossible to study. If you are interested to know more about them, you can use these terms to do further research on your own. However, do note that you need the guidance of a Vajrayāna teacher to gain a deeper understanding and to practice these techniques.

Annuttarayoga Tantras

In the Annuttarayoga Tantras, traditional Vajrayāna describes two stages of practice. The only way to understand such practices is through Buddhist teachers who have been certified to do so. However, to give you a general idea of these practices, there are two stages: Generation Stage and Completion Stage.

It goes without saying the Generation Stage is the initial stage. It is the time when one practices in deity yoga. This pertains to identifying one's self with the meditational Buddha in the form of visualizations. The aspirant would undergo guided meditation to concentrate on becoming "one" with the deity.

During the generation stage and while practicing the Deity Yoga, the aspirant would visualize the "Four Purities," which are the core of this stage. Do note that the Four Purities are exclusive to Vajrayāna, and it is what differentiates it from the other schools of Buddhism.

The Four Purities are:

1. Seeing one's body as the body of the deity,
2. Seeing one's surroundings as the Pure Land of the deity,
3. Perceiving one's pleasures as the blissfulness of the deity, free from attachment, and
4. Performing one's actions solely for the welfare of others – altruism.

After the Generation stage, the aspirant would then elevate to the Completion Stage. During this stage, he can choose to employ either the Path of Method or the Path of Liberation.

If the aspirant chooses the Path of Method (thabs lam), he will practice Kundalini Yoga, which taps into the body's energy system, specifically the *chakras* and the energy levels. Through Kundalini Yoga, one's "wind energy" is drawn towards the heart chakra, where it will be dissolved. Once this has been accomplished, the aspirant would then be transformed both physically and mentally.

If the aspirant chooses the Path of Liberation ('grol lam), then he would practice Mindfulness. Through this meditation, the aspirant would learn the truths of inherent Emptiness.

You have reached the end of our detailed discussion on the Four Schools of Buddhism. All aspiring Buddhists should not just familiarize themselves with these divisions, but also take the time to study each of them deeply. It is important to be constantly curious and to keep learning, especially when you are on a spiritual pilgrimage to find yourself and the path that will lead you to true Enlightenment.

I hope that this particular chapter has shed light on many of your questions regarding the different knowledge and practices of Buddhism. In the next chapter, we are to delve deeper into the general concept of Suffering.

CHAPTER 5

WHAT IS A SUFFERING?

"The source of all suffering is an attachment."

— The Buddha

Before we begin to talk about the meaning of Suffering in Buddhism, perhaps it would delight you to read about the Parable of the Poisoned Arrow first. The First Buddha himself told it to the monk Malunkyaputta.

It began when the monk Malunkyaputta was bothered as to why the Buddha remained silent on the Undeclared Questions. Such questions are concerned with the existence of the world in time and space, with personal identity, and with life after death. They are as follows:

Questions on the existence of the world in time:

1. Is the world everlasting?
2. … or not?
3. … or both?

4. ... or neither?

Questions on the existence of the world in space:

1. Is the world bounded in space?
2. ... or not?
3. ... or both?
4. ... or neither?

Questions about personal identity:

1. Is it self-indistinguishable from the body?
2. ... or is it dissimilar to the body?

Questions about life after death:

1. Does the Buddha exist after death?
2. ... or not?
3. ... or both?
4. ... or neither?

Because he cannot accept the Buddha's silence to these questions, he ventured forth to search for the Buddha himself in an attempt to obtain the answers to these questions. On meeting the Buddha, the Buddha told him that he never swore to explain the ultimate metaphysical realities such as those. Then, he shared with Malunkyaputta the Parable of the Poisoned Arrow to explain why such questions are not relevant to his teachings.

Here is the story:

> "It is similar to the situation in which a man would find himself pierced by a heavily poisoned arrow. His friends and comrades, family and relatives would offer him to a surgeon, but he would say, 'I will not have this arrow taken out until I find out if the man who shot me was a noble warrior, a priest, a merchant, or a laborer.'

> Then, he would continue by saying, 'I will not have this arrow taken out until I find out the first and last names of the man who shot me... until I find out if he was tall, medium, or short... until I find out if he had golden, reddish-brown, or dark skin... until I find out his home village, city, or town...

51

Until I find out if the bow that was used to shoot me was a crossbow or a longbow... until I find out if the bowstring that was used to shoot me was bark, sinew, bamboo threads, fiber, or hemp... until I find out if the shaft that was used to shoot me was cultivated or wild...

Until I find out if the feathers attached to the shaft that was used to shoot me were from a stork, a peacock, a vulture, a hawk, or some other fowl... until I find out if the shaft that was used to shoot me was held together with the sinew of a water buffalo, an ox, a monkey, or a langur.'

After that, the man would continue by saying, 'I will not have the arrow taken out until I find out whether the shaft that was used to pierce me was a curved arrow, a common arrow, a barbed arrow, an oleander arrow, or a calf-toothed arrow.

The man would then die from the wound but would never know the truths behind such queries."

Perhaps another reason why the Buddha told this parable is to reveal man's insatiability or *Dukkha*, which is the root of all suffering. Now, let us discuss *Dukkha* in detail.

The Three Categories of Dukkha

Buddhist teachings reveal the three types of Dukkha:

The first is the *Dukkah-dukka* or the dukkha of painful experiences. This category comprises of both the mental and physical sufferings associated with birth, aging, illness, and death. It refers to the pain experienced from what does not give pleasure.

The second is the *Viparinama-dukka* or the dukkha of the transforming nature of all beings. The experience of feeling frustrated because you are not getting what you expected, or desire best describes this category.

The third is the *Sankhara-dukkha* or the dukkha of conditioned experience. This is characterized by one's "basic insatiability" that is prevalent in all forms of life and all of the existence because all forms of life are ever-changing, never permanent, and without an inner substance or core. In other words, it refers to constant desire in a way that one's satisfactions and expectations can never really be met.

Multiple Buddhist teachings emphasize that life in the mundane world is dukkha. It does not just include birth, aging, illness, and death, but also feelings of grief, pain, worry, and despair. Being separated from one's beloved is dukkha just as much as being associated with one's enemy is. Whenever one does not acquire what one wants, it is dukkha.

The Five Clinging-Aggregates is an important Buddha concept with regard to dukkha as well. These are:

1. Form or Matter (rupa)

   The form of any sentient being or object is composed of the four elements: earth, water, fire, and wind (as mentioned in the second Chapter).

2. Sensation or Feeling (vedana)

   This refers to the experience of the senses of a being, which can be enjoyable, unenjoyable, or neutral.

3. Perception (samnjna)

   It is the mental and sensory process that notices, acknowledges, and labels. One uses perception to notice the feeling of happiness and anger, the size and color of plants and animals, and so on.

4. Mental Formations (samskara)

   These are every single kind of mental imprints and conditioning caused by any object. They also encompass any process that causes one to act on something.

5. Consciousness (vijnana)

   This refers to one's awareness of any object and the ability to distinguish its parts and features. Different Buddhist teachings explain Consciousness as:

   - Having a knowledge of something, or discernment (according to Nikayas/Agamas).

   - A set of interconnected discrete acts of discernment that changes quickly (according to the Abhidhamma).

   - The foundation of all experience (according to some Mahayana texts).

In a nutshell, one can safely say that suffering can be found anywhere and everywhere. You experience it whenever you feel attached to anything, be it your thoughts, words, actions, body, mind, loved ones, surroundings, and so on. The only way to be free from it is to follow the advice of the Buddha, and it is to practice the Noble Eightfold Path.

Now that you have gained further insight into the Buddhist concept of Suffering, you might be interested in learning more about Karma. Such a word is being thrown around carelessly by non-professionals in the modern world, but you will soon learn of its true meaning in the next chapter.

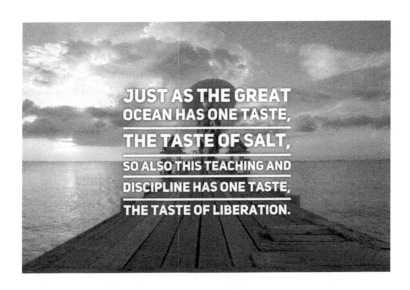

JUST AS THE GREAT
OCEAN HAS ONE TASTE,
THE TASTE OF SALT,
SO ALSO THIS TEACHING AND
DISCIPLINE HAS ONE TASTE,
THE TASTE OF LIBERATION.

CHAPTER 6

WHAT IS KARMA?

"Just as the great ocean has one taste, the taste of salt, so also this teaching and discipline have one taste, the taste of liberation."

— The Buddha

Strictly speaking, the meaning of *karma* refers to any action, intent, and deed by a being. It summarizes the spiritual tenet of cause and effect, wherein the actions and intentions of a being help shape the future of that being.

In a general sense, having good intentions and doing good deeds strengthen good karma and promote the possibility of happiness in the future. On the other hand, having bad intent and doing bad deeds can lead to bad karma and, hence, the possibility of experiencing pain and suffering.

In traditional Buddhism, *karma* specifically refers to action based on the being's intentions. Such intentions would then determine the being's cycle of rebirth. The word used to describe the "effect" of karma is *karmaphala*. You can think of *karma* as the seed and *karmaphala*as the fruit of that seed.

As mentioned in the previous sections, our karma is what keeps us "chained" to rebirth in the "mundane world." The Buddhist concept of rebirth is also called Reincarnation, and it is described in detail in the next chapter. For now, let us define it as the cycle of birth and death within the six realms of the mundane world, driven by ignorance, desire, and hatred. The only way out of this cycle is by following the teachings of the Buddha, particularly the Noble Eightfold Path.

Karma as a Process

According to the Buddha, karma is not an all-around determinant, but rather a part of the factors that affect the future, with other factors being circumstantial and in relation to the nature of the being. It moves in a fluid and dynamic way, rather than in a mechanical, linear manner. In fact, not all factors in the present can be attributed to karma.

Be careful not to define karma as "fate" or "foreordination." Karma is not some form of godly judgment imposed on beings that did good or bad things. Rather, it is the natural result of the process.

In other words, doing a good deed would not automatically entitle you to a future of happiness, and vice versa. After all, while certain experiences in your life are due to your actions in the past, how you respond to them is not yet determined. Of course, such responses to circumstances would then lead to their own consequences in the future.

Karma as Energy

All beings constantly change due to karma. For every thought, action, and word being produced, a kind of energy is released in different directions into the universe. These energies have the power to influence and change all other beings, including the being that sends the energy.

Think of the following scenario:

> Janice and Carrie work in the same office with three other people. Janice notices that Carrie is constantly late and contributes poor output to the team if any at all. Because of this, Janice is irritated at Carrie. Each morning, whenever she

sees Carrie at the office, she thinks, *Carrie is so annoying and incompetent. She should be fired.* After weeks of entertaining such thoughts, she then made the decision to talk to her three co-workers regarding Carrie.

One morning, before Carrie arrived, Janice approached her co-workers by the water dispenser and said, "I think Carrie is irritating. She doesn't do a good job, and she is always late." The other co-workers nodded and said that they agreed. After that, all four of them became hostile towards Carrie whenever she walked into the office. It was not long before their hostility drove Carrie to report them to the head office, who then called for a meeting regarding the issue.

With this story in mind, try to highlight the main energies that played a pivotal role in the fates of these office workers. Janice, the main character, experienced feeling irritated by Carrie's lack of professionalism at the office, which is a completely natural response, by the way.

This "energy" in the form of feeling then transformed into thoughts of annoyance (*Carrie is so annoying and incompetent…*) which Janice then deliberately transformed into another type of energy in the form of words ("I think Carrie is irritating…"). This new energy was then received by the three co-workers whose own thoughts, actions, and words became transformed due to the one that Janice sent to them.

Now, what is the point of all this?

It is to show karma in action in the modern-day setting. It does not necessarily mean that Carrie would be punished because of Janice's action, but it simply goes to show the power all beings possess, and it is their ability to send and receive energies.

The main reason why Buddhists emphasize the value of understanding karma is the fact that your knowledge of it will help you free yourself from samsara. Once you have recognized that every single intention and action you do may have an effect on your future, you become more mindful of your thoughts, words, and deeds. Ultimately, we are the ones in control of our future, but if we continue to be ignorant of our choices, then it would naturally lead to more suffering.

It's a good idea to try to think of all of our actions having karmic value because if you switch over to that philosophy, you start to head in a more positive direction. Your suffering and whether you continue in the endless circle really do depend upon what you learn in this life. Thus, using the idea of the three categories of Dukkha or suffering which were explained in the last chapter, you can take notes of which actions you feel you take that need to be changed, in order to limit your suffering.

Another exercise that is valuable is to try and work on the positivity of your energy. This can be worked on in all kinds of environments. Take the example of Janice that was shown earlier, and you can see how you control the energies of others as well as those that you feel. When you come across a situation which tempts you to use negative energy, try to look at it from another stance and think of a way in which you can use positive energy instead. Quite often the karma that lies in our actions comes from the actions taken and the amount of negative energy shared. Thus, it will always work in your favor, to be honest in your dealings with others and to try to raise your energy level above any negative experiences that you may encounter.

As you learn to discipline the mind, you also learn to control the karma that happens in your day to day life and that's huge. That means that you limit your suffering and are able to live with that high energy in a positive way that influences those around you to stay positive regardless of what difficulties they are faced with. The inner voice of calm that is able to control the voice of criticism and anger is one that helps you to become a human being who is able to work within the parameters of karma in a very positive light. That's important but you do need to make sure that your solutions are not so closed minded that they impinge upon the thoughts and energies of others.

IT IS IN THE
NATURE OF THINGS
THAT JOY ARISES
IN A PERSON FREE
FROM REMORSE

CHAPTER 7

WHAT IS REINCARNATION?

"It is in the nature of things that joy arises in a person free from remorse."

— The Buddha

When you think of the word reincarnation, what comes to mind?

Most people would think of it as the idea of dying and then resuming life once more on earth, but this time in a different form. For instance, if you were human in this lifetime, then depending on how good or bad you were, you could be reincarnated into a life of a king or a cockroach.

Unfortunately, such a misunderstanding of reincarnation has caused most people to shun all the other pertinent teachings of the Buddha. This problem may be because many have been misinterpreting many of Buddha's eighty-four thousand parables.

It should be noted that Buddha adopts a teaching style that is appropriate to the abilities of the learner, and during times when the people were accustomed to the simple way of life, he resorted to explaining his teachings in the form of stories. The Buddha had used the concept of being reincarnated into an animal to explain how one's ignorance ensnares one in the cycle of life and death. However, some who did not understand such a metaphor took the meaning literally.

Now, it is important to remember that reincarnation – rebirth – does not literally equate to the physical birth of a being. Experiencing rebirth does not mean that after death your consciousness is transferred to the fetus of a dog.

The True Meaning of Reincarnation

The term "reincarnation" (sometimes called "rebirth" in English books about Buddhism) does not have a direct translation in the languages of Sanskrit and Pali. Instead, traditional Buddhist teachings describe the concept using a variety of terms, but all of which represent the crucial step in the never-ending cycle of samsara. The terms Pali and Sanskrit are also termed *samsara which* means "wandering about," and it refers to the universal process of being reborn over and over again.

One such Buddhist term is *pubarbhava*, which literally translates to "becoming again." Another is *punarjanman*, which means, "re-born." Yet another one is *punarmrityu*, which translates to "re-death." Sometimes the simple word *bhava* – becoming – is used. However, the Pali and Sanskrit word for being born into the world in any way is *jati*, which literally means "birth."

One interesting paradox is in the minds of many people who do not fully understand the Buddhist concept of reincarnation. It is that one's soul transfers from one's dying body into a new one. However, the truth is that Buddhists do not actually believe that there is such a thing as a permanent "soul" within living beings.

According to Buddhism, a being – especially a human – is a combination of its thoughts, emotions, and perceptions that it then uses these as forms of energy to interact with the universe. In return, the universe sends back a reaction to these energies – *karmaphala*– that would cause a change in the person. Many Buddhists believe that such a transformation signifies that the person has become "born again" in the world of *samsara,* and the cycle continues.

The Ten Realms of Being

Concerning reincarnation in traditional Buddhism, there exist the Ten Realms of Being. Also known as the Ten Spiritual Realms, they represent the ten conditions of life which living beings experience each moment of their lives.

The Ten Realms of Being are comprised of Six Lower Realms of Desire, namely Hell, Hunger, Brutality, Arrogance, Passionate Idealism, and Rapture. The remaining are the Four Higher Realms of Nobility, namely Learning, Absorption, Bodhisattvahood, and Buddhahood. Buddhist modernists usually interpret these ten realms as states of mind instead of viewed in the literal sense.

Now, let us take a closer look at each of the ten realms. Perhaps you could even discover which one you are in right now.

The Six Lower Realms of Desire

Most sentient beings are trapped within these six lower realms. They do not move from one realm to another in a linear fashion, however, but in a more dynamic way depending on their karma and other factors.

Here are the six lower realms of desire:

1. Hell

   In traditional Buddhism, this realm is called the *Naraka*. In it, you experience a complete state of blind hostility. You feel as if you do not have the free will to choose how to act, in the sense that you seem ensnared in circumstances beyond your control.

   Those trapped in this realm are the ones who find it difficult to hold back their frustrations, anger, and hatred. They have the constant urge to destroy themselves and other beings around them. They see everything as threatening and hostile, so they feel claustrophobic towards their surroundings. Be warned, for it is difficult to escape from this realm.

2. Hunger

   Traditional Buddhists call this realm the *Pretas* or the world of the Hungry Ghosts. Those who are in this realm are the beings that have never-ending appetites coupled with extreme possessiveness.

61

Such negative qualities affect their thoughts and actions towards the source of their desire, be it power, fame, wealth, pleasures of the flesh, and so on. This "addiction" is never satiated; what is more, the level of desire heightens as soon as the being satisfies it.

Beings who are in this realm find it almost impossible to instill self-discipline. Their pursuit of pleasure affects them to the point where they no longer care for the welfare of other beings. This is a state that is easily understood by people today and is something that an individual can work on to try to correct the sense of need within themselves. Many learn from their own experience that the very core of their need is a manifestation of some kind of lack within their lives and does not add to the character at all. However, the lesson is a hard one to learn.

3. Brutality

This particular realm falls under the Buddhist World of the Animals. It is where the trapped being's thoughts and actions run on pure instinct, with no sense of morality. This means the being does not have sound reasoning and judgment.

Beings in the Brutality realm only live for the present moment, but not in the way that the Buddha teaches mindfulness. Rather, they take advantage of others for selfish reasons, not unlike how predators stalk and kill their prey in the wilderness. They also manipulate others in order to gain their favor and use them for personal gain. Again, one can work their way out of this state by understanding their own weaknesses and by learning to overcome them. Changes in the life of someone may signal a change of direction and this is needed to rise from this state, where the lack of morality is at the base of the problem.

4. Arrogance

In traditional Buddhism, this realm is described as the world of the demigods or the Asuras. Beings trapped here are those who are too engrossed in paranoid jealousy, the obsession to win, and paralyzing selfishness. Another distinctive quality of such beings is their constant desire to be on top in aspects of life they consider as important to them.

Although having such traits in the modern world may be considered beneficial, in the long term it destroys the being. This is because they value their own beliefs and ego more than the welfare of others. Being too competitive also holds the being back from being compassionate towards others, because they are considered contenders. It is good if you have things that you excel at, but you need to know the difference between being gifted and using the gift for the betterment of mankind and keeping the glory for yourself, seeing yourself as being the focal point. When you are gifted and accept that the gift you have can be used to help others, this helps you to overcome the part that ego takes in the equation.

5. Passionate Idealism

   In traditional Buddhist teaching, this realm falls into the world of the Humans. It is one where the beings have developed advanced thinking skills and discriminating awareness. The common trait in this realm is in being too ambitious with one's ideals.

   While this presents some benefits, especially as it can help motivate one to attain Enlightenment, it also leads to suffering due to the desire of attaining perfection. In the same way, we criticize people who try to be perfectionists because their self-criticism holds them back from ever achieving enlightenment. This sense of everything having to be perfect can stunt spiritual growth which is not a measurable thing and is therefore hard for perfectionists to understand. For example, when learning meditation, the perfectionist may try too hard and yet achieve very little. They need to let go of the need to be perfect in a world that is ever-changing and accept the changes that happen and become flexible toward them.

6. Rapture

   Traditional Buddhists associate this realm with the Buddhist world of the gods or the Devas. In this realm, which is sometimes referred to as the Heaven Realm, the beings experience short-lived, but strong feelings of pure pleasure.

   It cannot be avoided that beings only stay in this realm for a short time because the feeling of the rapture is momentary. Eventually, the being would then go back to a lower realm.

The Four Higher Realms of Nobility

The Four Higher Realms represent the traditional Buddhist tenet that sentient beings must exert all willpower and motivation to let go of their desires in the mundane world in order to understand the realities of nature and become their true selves.

The seventh and eighth realms – Learning and Absorption – are referred to as the "Two Vehicles" in Mahayanist Buddhism. This means that when a being finds himself in these realms, he is on the way to reaching the noblest realms.

However, because of the presence of desire and the focus on the self, specifically to increase one's wisdom and gain insight, then the being is still within the samsara.

7. Learning

    In traditional Buddhism, this realm is represented by the Sravakabuddha World or the realm of the Enlightened Disciples of a Buddha.

    In this realm, beings are in a state where they are seeking knowledge of the Truths and self-improvement by becoming learners. Specifically, they seek the guidance of a mentor or *guru*. Such guidance, if not coming from the guru himself, can be obtained from texts and other pre-recorded information.

    To come out of the lower realms and into this one, the aspirant should instigate the motivation to learn and to have an open mind towards the true nature of the world. This is a positive state to be in because you are receptive to the lessons you are being taught. You are also questioning and will find that gurus will give you examples to aid your understanding of life. This is a time when you may be reading a lot or going to classes in order to widen your knowledge and understanding of Buddhism.

8. Absorption

    This particular realm in traditional Buddhism is the World of the Pretyekabuddha, or "a Buddha on their own."

    Beings who have reached this realm are those who seek the truth based on their own observations and concentration. Typically, those who are in this realm have discovered that while external sources are indeed useful (as in the case of the Learning Realm), one's own learning experiences are truly superior. Therefore, beings that are in this realm have chosen to seek wisdom and truth through internal discernment.

This will apply to those who have learned to meditate and have the self-discipline to take that learning a step further. Once you do begin to learn and understand, this stage is one where you may improve your meditation to such an extent that you gain great understanding from it. You will be able to concentrate sufficiently to gain much from all that you are taught.

9. Bodhisattvahood

When the being has reached this realm, traditional Buddhists would state that he is in the World of the Bodhisattva.

As mentioned in the previous sections, the Bodhisattva are those who wish to become Buddhas in order to help other sentient beings find Enlightenment as well. Beings who have the compassion to commit themselves to helping other beings reach this realm. They experience pure bliss from not only having reached Enlightenment but also going on with their life guiding learners who are on their way. Being almost a stage of teaching, this higher state would apply to people who are willing to assist others to understand the teachings of Buddhism. This may apply to teachers within a Buddhist community who have proven awareness and who are able to help others to gain that same sense of awareness. There is no ego here. There is simply the need to pass on the learning to others so that they too may experience the most from their studies of Buddhism.

10. Buddhahood

The Enlightened One, The Buddhas, reside in this realm. Reaching this realm means experiencing pure, everlasting joy that cannot be influenced by any circumstances.

The Buddhas are free from all desire and suffering. Their wisdom, compassion, and loving kindness know no bounds. Because sentient beings who have reached this realm are so rare, it is not easy to describe. Generally speaking, it is no longer possible for those who have reached Buddhahood to descend to any of the lower realms because their happiness is no longer attached to external sources.

However, the Buddha explained that all living beings are capable of reaching this realm. This realm does not depend upon anything other than reaching Nirvana or total understanding and enlightenment and that's what people seek when they meditate, just as the original Buddha did. This is what people aim for through meditation and is the purpose of the journey into Buddhism.

I hope that this chapter has shed light on the Buddhist concept of reincarnation for you. At this point, you can reflect on certain aspects of your life, such as the realm in which you think you find yourself now. This helps you to aim higher – not for ambition's sake, but to improve who you are and to help others on their road too.

By understanding reincarnation, you can also be more mindful of your intentions, thoughts, and actions. Keep in mind that for each choice you make in this life, you then transport yourself to a different realm. To attain the higher levels, you may choose to seek constant inspiration from the teachings of the Buddha and to practice self-discipline and mindfulness. This means teaching yourself to be able to meditate and being mindful that the world around you is forever changing. You should be able to recognize the changes in yourself and improve upon your weaknesses as a student of Buddhism. There are always people who are willing to assist you in your journey but you need to have confidence in the people you choose to help you on this journey.

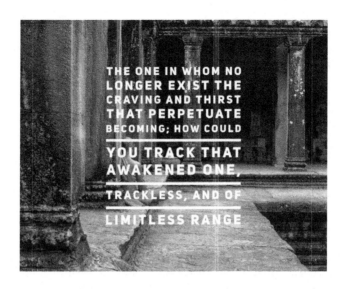

THE ONE IN WHOM NO
LONGER EXIST THE
CRAVING AND THIRST
THAT PERPETUATE
BECOMING; HOW COULD

YOU TRACK THAT
AWAKENED ONE,

TRACKLESS, AND OF

LIMITLESS RANGE

CHAPTER 8

WHAT IS NIRVANA?

"The one in whom no longer exist the craving and thirst
that perpetuate becoming; how could you track that
Awakened one, trackless, and of limitless range."

– The Buddha

Nirvana embodies the ultimate aspiration of Buddhists, which is to attain Enlightenment and be free from the cycle of samsara. In Buddhism, Nirvana is the state of the Non-Self (anatta) and of Emptiness (sunyata) because one is free from desire and self-centeredness. Many Buddhist scholars recognize two states of Nirvana, which are the "Nirvana with a Remainder" (sopadhishesa-nirvana) and the "Final Nirvana" (anupadhishesa-nirvana). The First Buddha is known to have attained both states.

The concept of Nirvana is one of the most fundamental elements within the Buddhist tradition, embodying the ultimate goal of the Buddhist practice. Despite its significance, it is not as cut and dry as the other elements within Buddhism. Shrouded in mystery, Nirvana is the source of endless speculation and even debate, creating significant differences between different schools of Buddhist ideology. While the basic concept of Nirvana is largely agreed upon specific details about its nature remain a matter left to individual belief. In the end, Nirvana is an aspect of Buddhism that serves to find common ground with many non-Buddhist traditions. However, it also serves to find a difference of opinion within the Buddhist community as a whole. In this light, Nirvana is one of the few actual mysteries to be found within the Buddhist tradition.

Perhaps one of the main reasons why Buddhism lacks mystery, in general, is the fact that the Buddha clearly defined the fundamental principles of Buddhism in his teachings. The Four Noble Truths break down the nature of life and suffering in such a basic way that there is little room for confusion of any sort. The basic idea that craving leads to suffering, and that the Eightfold Path will help a person to eliminate craving, and thus eliminate suffering, is about as simple and straightforward as it gets. The real problem is that the Buddha did not go into as great of detail when describing Nirvana as he did when describing everything else. To make matters even worse, Buddha did not encourage any real contemplation or speculation of Nirvana. Instead, the teachings of the Buddha place complete focus on the here and now and the actions that a person performs at this time.

The whole point of this focus was that by taking care of the here and now a person would arrive at Nirvana in due course. Thinking of Nirvana could actually be a dangerous thing. For one thing, the more time a person spends contemplating Nirvana is the less time they will spend focusing on the moment they are in. Since this is contrary to the basic principles of the Buddhist tradition, it makes sense that Buddha would not encourage such speculation. Additionally, if a person perfects their actions simply for the sake of attaining Nirvana, then a certain self-serving element enters the equation. As long as a person focuses on following the Eightfold Path simply for the sake of the Path itself then their actions are selfless. However, if the goal is to experience Nirvana, then there exists a hope for personal gain. Since personal gain leads to craving, then the idea of pursuing Nirvana becomes a very dangerous one indeed. As a result, Buddha said enough about Nirvana to make it a real aspect of Buddhist tradition, but not so much that it could become a hindrance to the other practices within the tradition.

The Basics of Nirvana

One of the aspects of Nirvana that can be agreed upon by everyone is the meaning of the word itself. Nirvana literally means 'cooling off' or 'blowing out'. While there are some debate and speculation over the precise reason why Buddha chose this word to describe a particular state of being it is generally agreed upon that it refers to the elimination of suffering. The craving and attachment (dukkha) that causes suffering in this life are often described as the fires of suffering. This same sense can be seen in modern terms outside of Buddhist traditions. Such terms as 'heat of passion', or 'fiery ambition' create the same images that the Buddha himself conveyed so many centuries ago. Since the Eightfold Path is the method by which a person can rid themselves of such passions and ambitions, it stands to reason that the end result of a successful journey on the Path would lead to those fires being extinguished. Thus, the terms 'cooling off' or 'blowing out' make perfect sense in the context of eradicating those things which cause suffering.

Another aspect of Nirvana, which almost everyone agrees upon is the sense that it is a destination to move toward. In terms of the Eightfold Path, this makes particularly good sense. After all, of what good is a path if it doesn't lead somewhere? Therefore, envisioning a state of existence that is free of the suffering associated with this life is a very necessary thing for anyone who wants to commit to following the Eightfold Path. Just as a person would be reluctant to drive down a street where they didn't know the outcome, so too, anyone would be hard-pressed to follow a path of life if they weren't at least somewhat sure of where that path would lead. Additionally, the fact that there are two basic paths leading to Nirvana is also largely agreed upon. The first path is that of the Eightfold Path. In this instance a person moves toward Nirvana in a gradual way, getting one step closer with each correct action that they take within the instruction of the Eightfold Path. The second path toward Nirvana is through enlightenment. This path can take a lifetime to achieve, just as the Eightfold Path, or it can happen instantaneously at any given time. Regardless of how or how quickly a person achieves enlightenment the one thing that is sure is that it will bring them to a state of Nirvana, even if only for a moment. And here is where the agreement on Nirvana comes to a virtual end.

Nirvana with a Remainder

According to ancient Buddhist texts, the Nirvana with a Remainder refers to the attainment of nirvana – freedom from samsara – within a single lifetime. This takes place when the Three Fires (Delusion or Confusion, Greed or Sensual Attachment, and Aversion or Ill Will) have been extinguished. However, there is still a "remainder" of the five Clinging-Aggregates, although this is merely ashes and no longer "burning." Richard Gombrich, a Buddhist scholar, defined the Five Clinging-Aggregates as the firewood that feeds the Three Fires. In order to stop fueling the Three Fires, the aspirant should make the effort to let go of the firewood. By doing so, one can reach the transcendent state which is Nirvana and become free from suffering, desire, and sense of self. Then, what remains is perfect happiness. Enlightened Ones who have attained Nirvana with a Remainder experience pure bliss and have a completely transformed and non-reactive mind that is free from any negative mental states. This is a very difficult concept for human beings to grasp because by making too much effort, you lose the ability to let go and this letting go helps you to grasp what it is that you need in order to reach Nirvana. We have miles to go before this becomes a concept that is clear enough to understand.

Nirvana with a Remainder is almost always the byproduct of enlightenment. It usually occurs without any sort of warning or expectation, just as enlightenment itself occurs. The fact that the Buddha achieved enlightenment after meditating for six years should not be taken for any sense of a normal time frame in which enlightenment is achieved. For a fortunate few, enlightenment can occur in a similarly short period of time, whereas for the vast majority of others it can take an entire lifetime or even longer to attain. No matter how long it takes to achieve enlightenment, it is a sudden and instantaneous experience. Much like turning on a light switch, enlightenment is both that quick and thorough. The state of being that enlightenment brings is a sense not so much of gaining knowledge, but more so of losing ignorance. An individual who experiences enlightenment feels as though they have lost a false sense of self and have been restored to a true sense of self. This ultimate sense of self affects how the individual relates to the rest of the world, and perhaps even the universe as a whole. This all-encompassing state of being is like being in a different world, although still being very much within the physical world as well. And this is the essence of Nirvana—a state of being which brings a person into a higher sense of oneness with all living things.

One of the advantages to Nirvana with a Remainder is that the person who achieves this state is able to share their experience with others. The Buddha himself is perhaps the first example of this phenomenon. After he reached enlightenment, Buddha devoted the remainder of his days to sharing his newfound knowledge with all who would listen. This also resembles the tradition of Jesus in a very real way. In fact, numerous traditions from around the world tell about a person going through a very real transformation and then spending the rest of their time helping others to achieve a transformation of their own. While it would be a large expectation to live up to the example of such great individuals the truth is that anyone who achieves Nirvana with a Remainder can, in fact, have a tremendous impact on the other people in their lives, helping to heal wounds of every type and ultimately guiding others on the path of self-discovery and eventual enlightenment. In this respect, the attainment of Nirvana is as though a person were able to get to Heaven without dying, and in turn, help others to get there as well.

Nirvana without Remainder

After learning about Nirvana with a Remainder, you most likely have an idea of what it means to attain Nirvana *without* Remainder. This is the final Nirvana wherein the Enlightened One is "blown out" at the end of his life; there is no fuel remaining. Another way of looking at this is the Buddhist equivalent of Heaven. Just as the Christian concept of Heaven involves a righteous soul attaining a higher state of being after being separated from their physical body through the process of death, so too, Nirvana without Remainder is the notion that the consciousness of the individual is fully released from the sufferings experienced in the physical realm through the process of death. This is the aspect of Nirvana that serves to unite Buddhism with certain non-Buddhist traditions. The idea of an afterlife paints an almost religious face of the Buddhist tradition, making it akin to Christianity, Islam, Judaism and numerous other traditions that hold firmly to a belief in a spiritual afterlife. However, this is also the area that perhaps creates the biggest difference between different schools of the Buddhist tradition.

One of the biggest issues with the idea of Nirvana as a type of afterlife is the aspect of a soul. Many Buddhist traditions don't actually believe in a soul the way that other traditions do. Instead of having a spiritual identity that goes from lifetime to lifetime a person is believed to simply be comprised of pure energy. The identity that forms in the person is the result of experiences encountered within a physical life. In this tradition, the notion of Nirvana is more like a person being 'relieved' of the ego and individual sense of self that necessarily kept them from being one with the divine source of life. Just as a drop of water in a glass ceases to be the ocean, so too, an individual being ceases to be a part of the divine whole. Nirvana is the experience of the individual's energy merging once again with the divine, becoming part of the whole once again, just like the drop of water being put back into the ocean where it can never be found again. True suffering in this tradition is the result of a sense of separateness from all other living things. Craving, attachment and the other sources of suffering are only extensions from the true cause which is a sense of separateness. By being freed from the physical experience of separation from the divine a person is subsequently freed from the fires of desire, craving, ego and the rest.

Another issue regarding Nirvana without Remainder is the aspect of reincarnation. While most other traditions that believe in a heaven of sorts would see this experience as the final destination, certain traditions within Buddhism believe that karma can, in fact, supersede Nirvana without Remainder. This basically means that even though an individual achieves Nirvana they are still expected to balance out any bad karma they may still possess. This bad karma can be from the life the person just lived, or it can be the karma from numerous past lives, still needing to be atoned for. And this is where it gets a bit tricky. If a person doesn't have a soul in the conventional sense, then how can they have karma from past lives? Additionally, if Nirvana is the ultimate freeing of a person from their individual state then how can they retain individual karma? Perhaps this is why the Buddha chose to focus on other aspects of life besides Nirvana. After all, who can truly know the answers to all of these questions?

Nirvana in a Nutshell

Despite the fact that many of these details can seem confusing and even contradictory, the prevailing belief is that a person who achieves Nirvana is not automatically released from their karmic obligations.

Some claim that a person with karma left to be resolved will not achieve the full measure of Nirvana. Rather, they will experience the transcendence and pure joy of it, but they will remain just below full integration with the divine source. Only when they have paid their karmic debt to the full will they be able to achieve total union with the divine source of life once again.

This underscores the true nature of Nirvana. Unlike the Heaven of Christianity or other such afterlife destinations, Nirvana is not seen as an actual location. Instead, Nirvana is seen as a state of being. This is why it can be achieved both before and after death. In the case of Nirvana with a Remainder, it is believed that a person can drift in and out of Nirvana, much the way that a person can go in or out of a room in their house. This is particularly true in the case of those who achieve Nirvana through enlightenment. While the Buddha achieved what could be termed 'enlightenment with a capital E', there are smaller 'doses' of enlightenment which could be termed 'enlightenment with a little e'. In the case of a lesser enlightenment, it stands to reason that the state of Nirvana achieved would potentially be temporary. Since other areas in that person's life remain in need of perfection, then they would be unable to experience full Nirvana. And since Nirvana is a state of being, then anything less than full Nirvana would necessarily be temporary rather than permanent.

Understanding Nirvana as a state of being can also serve to clear up the other elements that can make Nirvana seem so confusing. In this light, the experience of Nirvana after death can also be temporary. Just as a person achieving Nirvana while still alive may yet have lessons to learn, so too, a person experiencing Nirvana in death may still have lessons to learn or karma to balance. This can reconcile the notion of Nirvana and reincarnation to a reasonable degree of any mindset. Perhaps the best way to think of it is to imagine the Path as a path that is not flat but rather is hilly in nature. To experience a temporary Nirvana, in life or in death, can be seen as a person climbing a hill and seeing Nirvana in the distance. The sight of Nirvana can provide immeasurable excitement and inspiration, necessary things as they descend the hill and begin the next phase of the Path. Once Nirvana is well and truly reached, then there is no path left to travel, thus the person has reached the final goal.

Even then, however, a person can still choose to remain in the cycle of samsara, coming back in physical form to share their knowledge and love with those seeking a release from the suffering of the physical realm. This would explain the existence of such people as the Dalai Lama, who by all counts should have no outstanding karmic debts to be paid or any other lessons to learn that would bar him from total Nirvana. Traditions from all around the world speak of people who are somehow more than human, and this could be proof of such enlightened persons choosing to remain on this plane of existence in order to help humanity to achieve unity with the divine once again. Since Nirvana is not a location these people aren't really giving up as much as it might at first seem. Instead, they may simply be living in a state of full Nirvana even while taking physical form. And this is perhaps the biggest way in which Nirvana differs completely from any tradition of a heaven. Even though this life is seen as the means by which to achieve Nirvana, once Nirvana is achieved this life can still be lived, over and over again even. This is one of the most wonderful ways in which Buddhism is more than just a promise or a belief system. The fact that Nirvana can be achieved in this life, and constantly experienced in this life, means that there is no real distance between the physical and nonphysical realities. Subsequently, there remains one simple question regarding Nirvana. Is Nirvana more than simply the transformation of the individual? When enough people reach full Nirvana, if they remain on Earth could they affect a transformation of physical life as a whole? Can this entire realm experience the same transformation as the individual living in it? It seems the answer to that can only be revealed one person at a time.

CHAPTER 9

WHAT IS YOGA?

"Health is the greatest gift; contentment is the greatest wealth."

— The Buddha

In the modern world, Yoga has become synonymous with a type of exercise. However, the word itself holds so much more depth than that. The Sanskrit term *yoga* actually refers to an umbrella of physical, spiritual, and mental disciplines that began in ancient India.

Specifically, Yoga is a Hindu discipline that focuses on the training of the consciousness to attain perfect spiritual insight and tranquility. Practicing yoga involves taking three paths: the first is of actions, the second of knowledge, and the third of devotion.

In Buddhism, Yoga is in the form of meditation techniques that are focused on the improvement of one's mindfulness, discernment, and concentration. Some Buddhist aspirants practice yoga with the aim of attaining peace, tranquility, and even supramundane powers.

The presence of yoga in ancient Buddhist texts is strong, especially since meditation is a crucial part of the Noble Eightfold Path. There are two recognized types of yoga in Buddhism, and these are the *bhavana* and the *dhyana*.

Bhavana Yoga

In the Pali Canon, the term used to illustrate yoga is *bhavana*. The closest English word to bhavana is "development" or "cultivating." However, the former is more detailed as it indicates one's long-term personal and intentional motivation and effort in developing a specific aspect of one's life.

There are five general kinds of bhavana, namely:

1. The Development of Consciousness or Mind (Citta Bhavana),
2. The Development of Body (Kaya Bhavana),
3. The Development of Benevolence or Loving-Kindness (Metta Bhavana),
4. The Development of Understanding or Wisdom (Panna Bhavana), and
5. The Development of Concentration (Samadhi Bhavana).

To practice the Bhavana Yoga, you should choose which particular meditation object on which to concentrate. For instance, to develop one's mind, one must visualize one's present state of consciousness. To develop the body, one must also visualize the body as one meditates.

Bhavana is commonly taught by Yoga gurus to instill loving-kindness. It is also used to help cultivate positive thoughts and habits. Moreover, it is applied to enable the practitioner to visualize life occurrences.

For instance, those who wish to gain more wisdom can regularly meditate on images of them learning daily. This would then lead to a self-fulfilling prophecy, in which the practitioner actually goes out and does what he visualized doing.

Dhyana Yoga

The Sanskrit term *dhyana* (*jhana* in Pali) refers to meditation that will lead to the "state of perfect awareness and tranquility." According to some Buddhists texts, the practice of dhyana leads to the discernment of the Four Noble Truths.

In the Pali Canon, eight progressive states of dhyana are described. Four of these states are referred to as the "Meditations of Form" (rupa jhana) and the other four are the "Formless Meditations" (arupajhana).

The Meditations of Form

Each of the four dhyana has its own unique features, which are described below:

- First Dhyana

  The "Five Hindrances" (Chapter 4) are eradicated and replaced with pure bliss. Tender, subtle thoughts remain, but the mind no longer creates unwholesome intentions.

- Second Dhyana

  All mental processes cease, including the ability to create wholesome intentions. Only pure bliss remains.

- Third Dhyana

  Half of pure bliss dissipates, and what remains is tranquility.

- Fourth Dhyana

  Pure bliss dissipates entirely; therefore, the yogi can no longer feel pleasure or pain. Even one's own breath may stop for a moment. In traditional Buddhism, those who attain the fourth dhyana are said to acquire psychic powers.

The Formless Meditations

After attaining the four stages of the Meditations of Form, the yogi transitions to the Formless Meditations. These are the stages of the formless dhyana:

- Dimension of Infinite Space

  Upon reaching this state, the following qualities of the yogi are given much discernment: perception of the dimension of infinite space, contact, perception, singleness of mind, feeling, desire, consciousness, mindfulness, attention, decision, and persistence.

- Dimension of Infinite Consciousness

  The same qualities as in the Dimension of Infinite space are discerned by the yogi, but this time, it includes the perception of the dimension of the infinite consciousness.

- Dimension of Nothingness

  The same qualities are again discerned, but this time, it includes the perception of the dimension of nothingness.

- Dimension of Neither Perception nor Non-Perception

  At this point, none of the qualities is being discerned.

According to ancient Buddhist texts, an aspirant must not simply focus on reaching the higher dhyana. Rather, he is advised to master one dhyana at a time, before he moves on to the one above it. The mastery of a dhyana means you can enter into, stay in, and leave the state out of your own volition (in that there is no effort exerted). The problem that modern man has is that he is taught to make an effort and cannot easily understand that it is letting go of this effort that helps him to reach a state of better understanding. Thus, when mistakes are made during meditation, people have a tendency to self-criticize which is self-defeating. Instead, one needs to learn to continue on the same path, learning from the mistakes made that growth is possible through the mistakes, rather than letting them become a hindrance in the search for happiness.

CHAPTER 9 B

YOGA AS PHYSICAL MEDITATION

Yoga has become one of the most commonly practiced exercise routines in the world. Its popularity in the West cannot be overstated, with countless groups, styles, and schools to be found in the United States alone. Yoga has evolved into a practice that allows any individual the opportunity to exercise their body and mind in a way that helps to achieve many different goals. For some, Yoga is about conditioning the body, increasing flexibility, muscle tone and overall physical health. For others, Yoga is about stress relief, helping the individual to loosen tight muscles, breathe more deeply and attain a more relaxed state of physical and mental wellbeing. No matter what physical or mental needs you have, there is doubtlessly a yoga technique designed to specifically target those needs. Furthermore, yoga techniques have been developed for those with specific physical limitations, thereby allowing absolutely anyone to benefit from the centuries-old system that exercises both body and mind to create an overall state of happiness and wellbeing.

With the countless schools and groups that teach yoga comes numerous different yoga styles and techniques. This variety of systems closely resembles the various forms of martial arts developed over the centuries. While all yoga systems can trace their origins back to the original yoga systems practiced by the first yogis, they all possess a unique quality which makes them ideal for people with different strengths and different needs. Rather than being redundant, these various forms of yoga actually offer a very unique experience. As a result, it is important that you take the time to investigate the many different schools of yoga in order to determine which one is right for you. It is important to note that practicing yoga is a progressive experience, thus the form that is right for you as a beginner may not be right for you later on. This is another advantage to having so many systems to choose from. As you improve your yoga practice you can incorporate other systems that help you to grow both physically and mentally in completely new ways. A list of the 14 most common yoga styles is given below with a brief description of each. Further research on these schools can easily be done online.

Hatha Yoga

Hatha Yoga is an ideal system for anyone who is a beginner. The pace of the Hatha classes is slower than more demanding systems, allowing beginners the chance to learn the poses in a natural and progressive fashion. One of the main focuses of Hatha Yoga is breathing, which incorporates an element of concentrative meditation into the practice. Each position is held for a few breaths, allowing the practitioner the chance to fully engage in the position before moving on to the next. The name Hatha refers to the sun 'ha' and the moon 'tha', underscoring the importance of opposites. As a result, this form of yoga often pairs poses that affect different parts of the body, helping the practitioner to embrace the concept of opposites working together to create harmony. The slow rate of this system is ideal for reducing anxiety and stress as well as increasing flexibility and overall muscle tone. Additionally, the Hatha pace helps to induce a meditative quality, allowing the practitioner to enter the deepest parts of their mind while performing the poses.

Ashtanga Yoga

Ashtanga is a yoga system that is not for the faint of heart. Incorporating a more rigorous routine than Hatha Yoga, this system is more akin to a cardio workout routine than the gentle, peaceful systems that many pictures when they think of yoga. In fact, it is recommended that this system be abstained from, by women who are menstruating in order to maintain their vital energies. It is also recommended that the practitioner takes every seventh day off in order to allow their body to restore itself for the next round of sessions. Following a strict routine, this system is best performed in a professional setting with a trained instructor who can help you to get the postures and the sequences right. While practicing with an instructor means there will be others practicing alongside, this is still a very individualistic system. Rather than leading a class like an aerobics instructor does, the instructor will go from person to person ensuring that their technique is correct. Individual attention means that you can attend any class, regardless of experience. The length of a standard Ashtanga session can range between one and three hours, so it requires a great deal of commitment both in terms of time and effort.

Iyengar Yoga

Iyengar Yoga, otherwise known as 'furniture yoga' is a system that focuses on posture, alignment, and precision. Unlike other styles of yoga, Iyengar isn't practiced in an empty room with yoga mats. Instead, this system utilizes a variety of everyday objects, including chairs, blankets, blocks, and the like. Basically, this is the perfect form of yoga for anyone who doesn't have a lot of free space to work with! One advantage of this style is that the use of props allows people of all ages, physical type and overall ability to take part. Being able to lean on chairs takes away the need to be physically strong in order to perform certain poses. This is also an ideal form for anyone who is starting yoga and who isn't necessarily in the best physical shape. Since precision is of singular significance in this system it is more important that the practitioner get the pose right, even if it means using objects to help in the process. This also serves to reduce the risk of strain or overexertion, making this one of the safest systems of yoga for anyone with physical restrictions. The use of household objects in Iyengar Yoga makes this one of the best systems for anyone who has to practice at home.

Bikram Yoga

Bikram Yoga is a system that requires a professional yoga instructor and specific facilities. One of the main reasons for this is that Bikram Yoga is practiced in an environment where the temperature is 104°F and the humidity is at about 40%. These environmental conditions assist in detoxifying the body from harmful chemicals and toxins that can seriously impact a person's overall state of wellbeing. Bikram Yoga uses the basic Hatha system postures in a precise routine. This routine lasts for about 90 minutes and consists of 26 separate postures and two different breathing exercises. This system has elements of both Iyengar Yoga and Ashtanga Yoga. The focus on precision reflects the Iyengar system, while the strict routine reflects the Ashtanga system. Bikram Yoga benefits include improved muscle tone, greater flexibility, improved posture, increased focus and clarity of mind. This system is truly one of the best in terms of both mental and physical benefits. Due to the rigorous nature of this system, it is not recommended for anyone with certain health issues. Fortunately, qualified Bikram instructors will be able to advise you as to whether or not you are healthy enough for this system. In order to be a qualified instructor, a person has to complete a rigorous nine-week course. Therefore, their judgment will be well informed.

Yin Yoga

Yin Yoga is a system that focuses on increasing flexibility and joint strength. Originally developed as a yoga style for use with martial arts training, Yin Yoga is a perfect system for anyone who wants to increase their energy as well as their physical wellbeing. The founder of Yin Yoga, Paulie Zink, is a renowned martial arts expert and teacher of Taoist Yoga. This system reflects the Taoist tradition by honing the practitioner's qi energy, the energy that runs through the body and provides vitality, health and inner strength to a person. By enhancing the qi energy a Yin Yoga practitioner will see improvements in organ health, a stronger immune system, and an overall improvement in emotional and mental health. One way that the qi energy is enhanced is by clearing the path for it to travel, thereby helping it to reach all parts of the body with equal strength and vibrancy. Postures in this system help to improve overall circulation, especially to the joints, which is vital in increasing qi energy circulation. The way that this system differs from other systems is the length of time that the poses are held for. Instead of the traditional minute or so Yin Yoga requires the practitioner to hold a pose for a full five minutes or even longer. This is what affects flexibility the most, as the lengthy hold of a pose will assist in muscle development. It is advised that you practice this style with a professional instructor as the intensity of it could raise the risk of injury for the beginner.

Vinyasa Power and Flow Yoga

Like the name suggests, the Vinyasa Power and Flow system is a more upbeat and energetic style of yoga, resembling a cardio workout as much as a yoga routine. This style is very popular in the modern yoga community as it merges high tempo routines with the calming and meditative aspects of yoga practice. The main focus of this system is breathing, but instead of the focused, steady breathing of slower systems, this style is about the flow of breathing and motion in a faster-paced routine. In a way, this system is almost like choreographed dancing, putting pose after pose in quick succession, thereby improving the practitioner's breathing rate and technique. The high tempo nature of this system is also ideal for anyone who wants to break the proverbial sweat while performing their routine. The end result is a workout that improves heart rate, respiratory function, muscle tone and that offers a level of detoxification as well. Unlike other systems, the routines in Vinyasa Yoga are not strictly structured, therefore different instructors will use different techniques according to their personal preferences. Subsequently, you may find that you will want to try numerous different instructors before deciding which one offers a routine that you feel most comfortable with. One advantage to this is that you can change instructors from time to time in order to freshen up the experience a bit.

Kripalu Yoga

If Vinyasa Yoga is ideal for those who want to focus on the physical side of yoga then Kripalu is the system that is ideal for those who want to focus on the meditative side of yoga. Focusing on traditional yoga poses, breathing, relaxation and peace of mind, Kripalu is the style of yoga that you think of when you imagine a quiet, serene place where yoga practitioners are increasing their inward focus as they silently move from one elegant pose to the next. The Kripalu routine is divided into three separate stages, each with a specific focal element. Stage one is designed to focus on the physical aspect of the routine. Proper posture and the flow of breath and movement are the basic elements of this stage. Stage two focuses on the meditative aspect of the routine. A sense of connecting to the inner self is achieved by holding each pose for an extended time. Unlike Yin Yoga, the extended hold of poses in this system is more relaxed, allowing the practitioner to concentrate inwardly rather than on stretching muscles or increasing joint circulation. The third and final stage of the Kripalu routine blends the physical and meditative aspects of the routine into one. At this point, the practitioner experiences a unity between mind and body, with both seeming to move in one accord. This stage can also become somewhat expressive, whereby the practitioner is able to move to their own creative inspiration while following the instructor's overall guidance. One of the main features of Kripalu Yoga is the focus on compassion and a sense of self-acceptance as well as an acceptance of others. In this way, Kripalu is an excellent system for anyone who wants to incorporate the Eightfold Path into their yoga routine.

Jivamukti Yoga

Jivamukti Yoga is a more modern variation of yoga, incorporating education as well as meditation and yoga routines. The name Jivamukti is a variation on a Sanskrit word which means liberation while living. In this case, the liberation refers to the cycle of death and rebirth. Unlike other yoga styles, this particular style is more of an ongoing, varied experience rather than the same experience repeated week after week. Some weeks will see a focus on physically demanding routines, such as Vinyasa Power and Flow routines. Other weeks, however, will focus more on meditation or on other aspects of spiritual and mindful ideas and practices. Students, as well as instructors, can contribute to the general theme of the week, making this a very interactive format. One advantage of this style is that it incorporates virtually all other styles of yoga; therefore you can get a feel for different variations while practicing in one place with the same instructor. On the downside, the lack of routine may prove distracting, especially for anyone who prefers a stricter format for their practice. Additionally, Jivamukti schools are not as widespread as other schools, making them harder to come by. This is an ideal system for anyone who wants a more interactive and wide-ranging spiritual experience.

Kundalini Yoga

Another relative newcomer to the yoga community is the system known as Kundalini Yoga. As the name suggests, this system focuses on the awakening and nurturing of the Kundalini energy. In order to obtain this goal, the Kundalini system has developed a routine that utilizes yoga poses, mantra chanting, meditation and proper breathing, or pranayama. As a result, Kundalini Yoga is often called the 'yoga of awareness' by its practitioners. The overall aim of Kundalini Yoga is to unite the three basic aspects of a person—body, mind, and soul. Kundalini Yoga is divided into six separate parts, each with a specific goal and routine. The first part involves mantra chanting. This allows the practitioner to shift their mental focus away from outside thoughts and toward the yoga routine itself. The second part involves breathing exercises. This allows the practitioner to get their breathing deep and relaxed. Part three is a series of exercises known as Kriya. These exercises combine yoga poses, breathing techniques and sounds, including mantra chanting. Part four is comprised of relaxation techniques, allowing the body and mind to unwind and rest after the Kriya routines. The fifth part consists of meditation exercises. This helps the practitioner to focus inward and connect with their inner self. Finally, part six is the closing ritual which consists of a blessing chant or song. This six stage system is ideal for anyone looking for something that closely resembles a spiritual ritual of sorts. A session will ordinarily last between 60-90 minutes, however, this is subject to the instructor and shorter classes or longer classes can often occur.

Anusara Yoga

The Anusara system of yoga is one of the newest systems in existence. Developed in 1997 by the American yoga instructor, John Friend, this system is a hybrid of Iyengar Yoga and Hindu spiritual traditions. One of the defining qualities of this school is the fact that practitioners are encouraged to virtually 'do their own thing'. This doesn't mean that the room turns into uncontrolled chaos, instead, it means that each practitioner can turn their yoga routine into an interpretive exercise, allowing them to express their feelings and desires through the series of poses they perform. The main reason for this approach is to keep the practice of yoga unique for each person. Rather than transforming the practitioner into a set mold the Anusara system allows each person to develop along their own path. The three focal points of the Anusara system are attitude, alignment, and action, otherwise referred to as the three A's. The Hindu element of these classes can be seen in the opening stage, which consists of three chants of Om, three sets of opening invocations, and a final chant of Om. All in all this style is ideal for anyone who wants a more relaxed environment that offers a relatively even mix of structure, individual freedom, and spiritual comfort.

Viniyoga

Viniyoga is another system that focuses on the individual rather than on a specific set of activities and routines. While the poses are rooted in the basic yoga tradition, they are adapted to suit the specific abilities and needs of the practitioner. Unfortunately, the name Viniyoga has nothing to do with the French "vin" (meaning wine)! Rather, Viniyoga gets its name from the word Vini which can be translated as adaptation, differentiation, and application. The primary focus of this system is to safely improve muscle tone. A practitioner of Viniyoga will go through the extra steps of warming up a muscle and then contracting the muscle before beginning the stretching exercise. This practice results in the muscle being better prepared for each yoga pose, thereby significantly reducing the risk of straining or tearing. Viniyoga can be an ideal style for anyone who is going through physical rehabilitation or who is at greater risk of muscle damage during regular exercise. The one downside of this system is that it lacks the meditative and spiritual qualities of many of the other systems.

Sivananda Yoga

The system of Sivananda Yoga is a great system for anyone who is new to yoga. With a slower, unrushed pace, the Sivananda system is an ideal way to learn the basic yoga poses and to develop a general understanding of the overall yoga philosophy. As a general rule, the Sivananda routine sticks to the same 12 basic yoga poses, or asanas, with only slight variations occurring. This is ideal for first-time practitioners who might find other systems a bit overwhelming at first. In addition to the physical element of yoga, Sivananda also promotes a five-point philosophy that enables the practitioner to incorporate the practice into their day to day lives. The five points of the philosophy are proper breathing, proper diet, proper exercise, relaxation and a positive state of mind. This system is ideal for anyone who wants a basic yoga routine that also incorporates a general sense of mental and spiritual wellbeing. This is also an ideal system for anyone who has physical restrictions which might make other systems too demanding.

Restorative Yoga

Like Iyengar Yoga, Restorative Yoga is a system that allows the use of objects for the sake of support while performing the different yoga poses. The main point of this system is to promote healthy exercise without unnecessary stress or overexertion. Most of the poses incorporated in Restorative Yoga are seated postures, meaning that they are less demanding than the poses used in other systems. Furthermore, the use of objects such as blankets, blocks and the like allow the practitioner to focus on the pose without having to be in perfect physical condition. If you want a yoga system that is calming and relaxing, then this is probably the best system for you. Additionally, this style is ideal for anyone who is going through physical therapy or rehabilitation, as it has a relaxed rate which is beneficial for restoring strength to mending limbs or any other parts of the body recently affected by trauma. It is also a system that can be practiced at home without any danger of injury or distress.

Prenatal Yoga

Needless to say, unless you are an expecting mother, then this system is not one that is necessarily right for you! Prenatal Yoga is a system of yoga poses that has been carefully designed to help pregnant women during all stages of pregnancy. This provides a great deal of physical strength and suppleness which benefits any mother during and even after pregnancy. The demands placed on the body are compensated for in the routines of Prenatal Yoga, helping the mother to avoid the stress and potential overexertion on muscles that pregnancy can cause. Additionally, the Prenatal Yoga system will help a woman to recover strength and flexibility after giving birth, thereby enabling them to return to a normal life sooner and safer than would otherwise be possible. Prenatal Yoga can be performed anywhere, even at home, which makes it ideal for anyone expecting or with a newborn that they cannot leave unattended.

CHAPTER 9 C

BASIC YOGA POSES

Attaining unity between body and mind is one of the highest goals of the Buddhist practice. Over the years, exercise routines have been developed to help achieve this unity. These exercises have been collected and refined to form the basic yoga poses practiced around the world today. While yoga poses can be used to strengthen and purify the body alone, they can also be used to great effect in strengthening and purifying the mind as well. Some of the poses can actually be used in conjunction with meditation, creating a holistic approach to spiritual growth. Whether you are looking for exercise alone, or you want to find a practice that can offer more, yoga poses can prove to be the answer. Listed below are 13 of the more basic yoga poses with a brief description of their form, the benefits they provide and easy to follow steps that will enable you to practice them for yourself. Also included are some warnings regarding physical conditions that might pose a risk for certain poses. If you have any injuries or physical conditions it is **TOTALLY** recommended that you seek advice from a medical professional as well as a trained, certified yoga instructor. Additionally, it is also advised that you begin practicing in a supervised environment, either with a partner or an instructor. Once you get a feel for yoga you will be able to practice on your own without any problem whatsoever.

Corpse Pose

The Corpse Pose is considered one of the most relaxing of all yoga poses. It consists simply of you lying on your back with all of your limbs relaxed. Unfortunately, despite the simplicity of the final position, there are several steps to go through before achieving the final pose, making this one of the more complex poses for beginners. Benefits of this pose include relaxation, lower blood pressure, increased energy, relief of tension and tension headaches and mental calm, which can reduce stress and even some forms of mild depression. The steps for the Corpse Pose are as follows:

- Begin by sitting on the floor in a relatively neutral position. Place your feet soles down in front of you with your knees bent. Gently lean back onto your forearms. Place your hands on the floor and gently push down, lifting your pelvis slightly off the floor. Immediately relax your pelvis back onto the floor. Then lay on your back keeping your lower back slightly arched. Take in a slow deep breath while extending your right leg, then your left leg, pushing through your feet as you do. Relax your leg muscles, leaving your legs angled apart at a natural angle. Keep your feet turned out in a natural and relaxed way.

- Place your hands behind your head and gently press your head forward, stretching the muscles in the back of your neck to release tension.

- Stretch your arms up toward the ceiling. Rock gently from one side to the other, stretching the muscles in your shoulders. Slowly rest your arms on the floor, turning your arms to face outward with the back of your hands on the floor. Use this position to stretch the muscles in your collarbone. Then relax your arms into a normal pose.

- Remain in this pose for 5 minutes at a time. It is recommended that you use this pose once every 30 minutes during a regular yoga routine in order to relax your muscles and prevent strain. Take this opportunity to also breathe deeply, thereby relaxing your internal organs.

While this pose is meant for relaxation and muscle care, it is no less demanding than any other pose. Be sure to take plenty of time to perform it properly. In the case that you have discomfort in your neck or back while lying on the floor, you can use a towel or a pillow to ease the discomfort. Also, keep your knees bent in the case of lower back strain. The Sanskrit name for the corpse pose is Savasana. This is a level 1 yoga pose.

Easy Pose

It would perhaps be more accurate to call this pose the 'easy-ish pose' as it isn't really as easy as it sounds! The form of this pose is sitting upright, cross-legged, with your arms falling naturally, hands resting palms-down on your knees. While the Easy Pose may simply look like you are sitting in a natural position it will actually challenge anyone with bad posture. Needless to say, it is imperative that you take your time and concentrate while performing the Easy Pose. The benefits of the Easy Pose include stretching the lower joints, strengthening the muscles in your back, and even calming the mind. Steps for the Easy Pose are as follows:

- Place a folded blanket onto the floor to act as a comfortable cushion to sit on. It should be folded in such a way as to make the blanket about 6 inches high. Sit toward the edge of your blanket and stretch your legs out in front of you (this will resemble the Staff Pose).

- Cross your legs at the shins, widening your knees, and gently place each foot under the opposite knee, pulling your legs close to your center of gravity. In short, get into a cross-legged seated position.

- Relax any tension in your feet, allowing them to rest on the floor in a comfortable manner. The arches of your feet should rest against each shin. Your legs should form a neat triangle when viewed from above, with a gap between the feet and your pelvis. Do not pull your ankles inward.

- Make sure your pelvis is neutral, with no strain in it whatsoever. To find this position simply press your hands on the floor and lift your backside off the floor slightly, take a few breaths and lower your backside back down, letting it rest naturally.

- You can place your hands on your lap, however, most people allow them to rest on their knees as this can help the arms to release tension. Arch your back slightly to relieve tension and to ensure that you are in proper alignment. Take deep long breaths while in this position, allowing each exhale to release tension from your body and mind.

- This position can be held for as long as you like. It is a particularly popular pose for many forms of meditation. If you remain in the easy pose for a long period, it is recommended that you switch the positions of your legs to prevent cramping or any other discomfort. Alternatively, you can stretch one leg out at a time, keeping the other bent, thereby stretching your leg and lower back muscles.

Again, while this position is designed as a relaxing pose there are things to consider before trying the Easy Pose. If you have any knee injury or lower back issues, then you might want to skip this pose. At the very least consult a professional before attempting the pose. First-time practitioners may want to do this pose with their back against a wall in order to help establish proper posture and overall alignment. The Sanskrit name of the Easy Pose is Sukhasana. The Easy Pose is a level 1 yoga pose.

Cow Pose

If there is a yoga pose that deserves to be called the 'Easy Pose' it is unarguably the Cow Pose. This pose consists of you being on all fours with your back gently arched and your head facing forward. It is one of the gentlest poses on the body, placing no real strain on any joints or muscles. Another big advantage to this pose is that it can be a progressive one. In other words, you may find it difficult to arch your back and keep your head upright at first, but you can practice the pose in a way that works for you, gradually increasing your flexibility and muscle tone to where you can perform the pose perfectly later on. This pose offers the benefits of stretching your neck and front torso muscles while also providing a soothing massage effect to your spine and lower organs. Steps for the Cow Pose are as follows:

- Begin by getting on all fours. Your knees should be in a straight line below your hips. Your hands, elbows, and shoulders should form a straight line and be perpendicular to the floor. At this stage, you can keep your head in a relaxed position with your eyes facing down toward the floor.

- Take in a deep breath and lift your backside and chest upward, toward the ceiling. Allow your stomach to drop down toward the floor in a naturally relaxed way. Do not clench your stomach. Gently raise your head so that you are looking straight ahead.

- As you breathe out, you can relax your head and chest, returning

91

to a classic 'tabletop' position. This routine should be repeated 10-20 times.

- When you have mastered this pose you can integrate it with the cat pose on the exhale, thereby creating a more fluid motion.

In the event that you have any neck injury, you can adapt this pose as needed. Keeping your head facing down is perfectly acceptable in these circumstances. Additionally, you can reduce the amount of lifting you do if you have any back issues. Always consult a professional in the event that you have any physical restrictions. The Sanskrit name for the Cow Pose is Bitilasana. This is a level 1 yoga pose.

Downward Facing Dog Pose

The Downward Facing Dog Pose is probably one of the most commonly practiced of all yoga poses. The main reason for this is that it provides your whole body with a stretch that rejuvenates and restores tired and sore muscles. Because this pose affects the whole body it has a wider range of benefits than just about any other yoga position. These benefits include strengthening muscles in the arms and legs, releasing tension from shoulders, calves, strengthening the arches of your feet, hamstrings and hands, improvement of digestion, lowering of blood pressure, relief of headache and back pain, reduction of fatigue, asthma and sciatica, restoring of energy, and relief of mild depression and moderate stress and anxiety. The complexity of this pose makes it one that is best done with a partner or a professional instructor. It can, however, be performed alone if you cannot find anyone to practice with. The steps of the Downward Facing Dog Pose are as follows:

- Begin by getting on all fours. Your knees should form a straight line below your hips, but your hands should be just forward of your shoulders. Make sure your hands are flat with your fingers pointing forward or slightly angled outward from your body. Turn your toes under in order to lift your knees in the next step.

- Slowly breathe out while lifting your knees off of the floor. Keep your heels off the floor and your knees bent slightly. Stretch your tailbone away from your pelvis and push gently forward. At this point raise your sitting bones upward, stretching your leg muscles as you do.

- With your next exhale place your heels on the floor, bringing your thighs back in the process. Gently straighten your knees at this point, but be sure not to lock them. Tighten your outer thigh muscles and gently roll your upper thighs inward.

- Tighten your outer arm muscles and press your index fingers flat against the floor. Stretch your inner arm muscles from your fingers to your shoulders, stretching your wrists as you do. Bring your shoulder blades back and in, then broaden them and press them toward your tailbone. Keep your head between your upper arms as you perform this move. Be sure not to let your head droop.

- Maintain this pose for between 1-3 minutes at a time. When you want to rest you can exhale and bring your knees slowly to the floor, forming the Child's Pose. You can choose to repeat the process if you wish.

Due to the all-inclusive nature of the Downward Facing Dog Pose, you should be aware of any physical restrictions before attempting to perform the pose. Pregnant women should refrain from this pose in late term, and anyone suffering from carpal tunnel syndrome or diarrhea should also refrain from performing this pose. If you have high blood pressure you will want to support your head to keep it more upright. Straps and blocks can be used to make the pose easier, but be sure to use these with the supervision of a trained instructor. As mentioned before, this pose is best done with a partner or instructor, especially if you are a beginner. The Sanskrit name for this pose is Adho Mukha Svanasana. The Downward Facing Dog Pose is a level 1 yoga pose.

Happy Baby Pose

When you perform the Happy Baby Pose you will completely understand how it got its name. This pose will have you on your back with your legs tucked in, knees bent and your hands holding onto your feet. While this pose may look easy it is, in fact, a fairly challenging pose as it requires a great deal of flexibility, especially around the hips. This is the type of flexibility babies are renowned for! The benefits of the Happy Baby Pose include relief of stress and fatigue, stretching of the back muscles and a gentle stretch of the groin muscles. It also serves to improve knee and hip health. The steps of the Happy Baby

Pose are as follows:

- Lay on your back. Be sure to use a mat or a blanket to prevent discomfort. Take in a deep breath. Slowly exhale, bending your knees and pulling them into your chest.

- Take in another deep breath, grasping your feet with your hands while you do so. Spread your knees so that they reach out just beyond your torso. Gently bring them upward toward your armpits.

- Bring your ankles directly over each knee, forming a straight line upward away from your torso. Your shins should be directly perpendicular to the floor. Press your feet upward into your hands, pulling your hands back simultaneously in order to create resistance. Hold this resistance for a deep breath or two before releasing. Repeat as many times as you wish.

Again, this pose looks a lot easier than it is, especially for beginners. In the event that you have troubles grasping both feet at the same time, you can use a strap. Be sure to keep the strap in the arches of your feet to avoid slipping. If you have any neck injuries or restrictions you can use a folded blanket to give your head additional support. This pose should be avoided by anyone who is pregnant or who has knee injuries. The Sanskrit name for this pose is Ananda Balasana. This is considered a level 1 yoga pose.

High Lunge Pose

Sitting for long periods of time can have very detrimental effects on your body. Fortunately, the High Lunge Pose is designed to target the areas most affected by sitting for long periods and help restore their health, flexibility, and vitality. Other physical benefits of the High Lunge Pose include relieving sciatica, relieving constipation and even curing indigestion. The name of this pose sounds like something straight from the gym and, truth-be-told, this pose is more akin to full-fledged exercise than many other level 1 yoga poses. When you are in this pose you will look as though you are at the starting line of a race, with one leg stretched out behind you while the other leg is bent at the knee, forming a straight line with your arms that are pointing straight down from your shoulders, with your hands on the floor. Your head will be somewhat elevated, but not looking straight ahead. This is a perfect pose for stretching arm and leg muscles, thereby improving muscle tone and restoring proper blood flow to those areas. This pose will also stretch the groin muscles, which can suffer total neglect from long periods of inactivity due to sitting. Steps of this pose are as follows:

- Stand on the floor and reach down to your ankles, pulling your abdomen in as close as possible to your legs. In the event that you cannot reach your ankles comfortably, you can keep your knees slightly bent, or simply reach down as far as you can. Bend your knees and, while breathing in, stretch your left leg straight behind you so that your left foot reaches the edge of your yoga mat. The ball of your left foot should be squarely on the floor. Make sure that you stretch your leg back far enough so that your right knee forms a 90-degree angle, forming a straight line between the floor and your right shoulder.

- Lower your torso onto your front thigh (in this case the right thigh) and stretch it forward. Look forward as much as possible while doing this as this will help you to keep the right alignment. Stretch your left leg out, bringing your left heel as close to the floor as possible.

- Breathe out and place your right foot back next to your left foot. Now bring your left knee forward and repeat the exercise, this time with your right foot stretched out behind you.

This pose is pretty straightforward, so it is one that can be safely practiced alone if need be. A block can be placed between the floor and the outstretched leg to help you hold the pose for a longer period of time. That said, it is important to make sure that you don't overstretch your muscles, or keep the pose for too long in order to prevent strain or injury to your muscles. This pose, when done right, should provide a soothing and restorative effect to your leg and arm muscles. Avoid this pose if you have any significant knee injuries or any neck issues that would make this pose potentially hazardous. In the case of any physical restrictions always consult a professional before attempting any of these poses. The High Lunge Pose is a level 1 yoga pose.

Hero Pose

Fortunately, you don't have to be a hero in order to be able to perform this pose. The Hero Pose is another seated pose that is ideal for resting your legs and can be performed during a regular yoga routine in order to provide an opportunity to rest and catch your breath or it can be performed on its own at the end of a long, busy day in order to soothe and restore your tired legs. Another application for the Hero Pose is an alternate sitting position for meditation. When done right, this pose will have you seated on the floor with your legs going straight back at the knees, with your feet facing up either side of your posterior. Your arms will go at a 45-degree angle to your knees, with your hands comfortably resting on the fronts of your knees. Your back will be straight and your head will be facing forward, ensuring proper posture. Despite the seated aspect of this pose, there are a great many physical benefits to be had by performing the Hero Pose. These benefits include relieving indigestion and gas, stretching your ankles, knees, and thighs, strengthening the muscles in your arches, reduction of leg swelling due to pregnancy, lowering blood pressure and relieving the symptoms of asthma. Steps for the Hero Pose are as follows:

- Begin by kneeling on the floor. Be sure to use a mat in order to prevent discomfort on a hard floor. Additionally, a folded blanket can be placed between your thighs and calves to help you to keep the proper distance between your legs with minimum effort. When you kneel, keep your thighs straight up and place your knees together. Gently slide your feet apart so that they extend just beyond your hips, keeping the tops of your feet flat on the floor. Point your big toes slightly inward, as this will help keep your feet flat on the floor.

- Take a deep breath in and slowly exhale. As you exhale sit back halfway, keeping your torso in a slightly forward leaning angle. Place your thumbs firmly behind your knees and rub down the back of your legs, pushing the skin and muscles toward your heels. Next, gently sit on the floor just between your feet.

- In the event that this position is uncomfortable, you can use a block or a book to sit on, thereby providing firm support while raising you up to a more comfortable position. Ensure that you are sitting evenly balanced. Rotate your thighs slightly inward, pressing your thigh bones into the floor with your hands. Now rest your hands in your lap facing up, or on your thighs facing down.

- Bring your shoulders back and sit up as straight as you can. Then release the tension from your shoulders and stretch your tailbone downwards, toward the floor.

- This pose should initially only be held for about 1 minute. However, as you get used to this position you can increase it to a full 5 minutes. When you are ready to come out of the pose simply place your hands on the floor and push yourself gently up. Bring your ankles under you and stretch your legs out directly in front of you. You can bounce your knees up and down a bit to release any tension in your legs.

Despite being a seated yoga pose the Hero Pose is not ideal if you have certain medical conditions. Anyone with heart problems should avoid this pose, as well as anyone with knee injuries or ankle issues. If you are suffering from a headache this may not be an ideal pose to use. As always, if you have physical restrictions, be sure to consult a proper instructor before attempting this pose on your own. Beginners can use a rolled up blanket or towel under their ankles to provide extra comfort and support. Practicing this pose with a partner can be beneficial as another person can help to ensure that your alignment is proper, thereby enabling you to get the full benefit of the pose. The Sanskrit name of the Hero Pose is Virasana. This is a level 1 yoga pose.

Legs-Up-the-Wall Pose

One thing that many yogis tend to do is to spend time either fully upside down, such as in a headstand, or partially upside down, such as in a pose similar to this one. The reason for this is that it is believed that inversion is highly beneficial for the body and that it can actually provide relief and even curative powers for just about any physical ailment. Therefore, the Legs-Up-the-Wall Pose is one of the most beneficial yoga poses for providing energy, pain relief, stress relief and a whole host of other physical and mental benefits. While this pose does offer some level of difficulty it is for the most part easy to perform. One of the great advantages of this pose is that it utilizes a wall or similar structure for support, thereby relieving you from the burden of keeping your legs held upward. Additionally, support is also provided under your back, helping you to find the perfect position where your body can be totally relaxed. Done properly, you will be on your back, legs straight, resting on a wall at about a 20-degree angle, or at a natural, relaxed angle. Your arms will be flat on the floor at about a

45-degree angle, again providing a natural, relaxed position, and your hands will be facing up. In short, you will look as though you fell down with your legs still sticking up!

As stated before, the physical and mental benefits of this pose are numerous. These benefits include relieving migraines, curing insomnia, relieving mild forms of depression, reducing stress and anxiety, aiding digestion, relieving arthritis, improving respiratory function, reducing varicose veins, reducing the effects of menopause, aiding in urinary function and health and improving circulation. Steps for the Legs-Up-the-Wall Pose are as follows:

- First, you will need to determine a few things in order to get your positioning right. If you are tall you will want to position yourself a little further away from the wall than if you are short. If you are flexible then your back support will be higher and closer to the wall, whereas if you are stiffer in nature than your support should be lower and further away from the wall. This is something you will want to play around with until you find what feels most natural and comfortable for you.

- Begin by sitting on your support, placed about 6 inches from the wall. You will begin by sitting sideways to the wall with your right side touching the wall. Take in a deep breath and slowly exhale. As you exhale you should raise your legs onto the wall while lowering your back and head onto the floor and turning so that your legs are flat against the wall and your torso is perpendicular to the wall. This movement will become more fluid and balanced the more you practice it.

- Your backside should be between the support and the wall, with your tailbone resting just under the support. Ensure that your torso has a slight arch to it, adjusting your support if needed to achieve this. Press your feet against the wall while bending your knees to lift yourself off of your support if you need to adjust it. Lower yourself gently once the adjustment is made.

- Raise your head slightly and lower it again, working out the stress from the base of your skull. Release any tension in your neck and throat. You can place a folded or rolled towel under your neck to add additional support. Stretch your shoulders upward while laying your arms comfortably at your side with your palms facing upward.

- Make sure that your legs are firm enough to maintain proper positioning. Next, release any tension in the rest of your body, literally allowing yourself to 'sink' into the floor. Turn your eyes downward as though you are looking at your chin, keeping them relaxed as you do so.

- Remain in this position for as long as you wish. When beginning you will be able to hold this position for about 5 minutes, but over time you will be able to hold it for as long as 15 minutes. Be sure to lower yourself down from this pose slowly and gently, bringing your legs down by rolling over onto your side. You should remain on your side for a couple of minutes, breathing deeply, allowing your body to reorient itself.

While this pose offers one of the largest lists of benefits it also has one of the longer lists regarding warnings. If you have eye troubles, such as glaucoma, then you should consult a physician before performing this pose. Additionally, if you have knee problems, back problems, neck problems or other physical restrictions, be sure to consult a professional. This pose is very similar to inversion style therapy and therefore should be treated with the same considerations. Fortunately, this pose can be modified to accommodate most physical conditions, so you should be able to benefit from the curative powers of the Legs-Up-the-Wall Pose even if you have some of these areas of concern. The Sanskrit name of this pose is Viparita Karani. This is a level 1 yoga pose.

Extended Puppy Pose

The Extended Puppy Pose is a welcome sight for any yoga practitioner as it is a pose designed for relaxation and restoration. This pose is a mix of the Downward Facing Dog Pose and the Child's Pose. When you perform this pose properly, you will be on your knees with your arms stretched out in front of you, your hands flat on the ground facing down and your head facing the floor with your chin almost touching the floor itself. Your thighs and torso will form a 45-degree angle, creating a right triangle with the floor and making this pose a favorite for geometry lovers! This is a simple pose, intended to stretch the muscles in the spine and shoulders, thereby providing a virtual massage. The Extended Puppy Pose is ideal for soothing the body and mind at the same time and can be done during a yoga routine or simply at the end of a busy, hectic day when the calming powers of this pose are very much needed. The steps for the Extended Puppy Pose are as follows:

- Get onto all fours, ensuring that your wrists are directly below your shoulders and your knees are directly below your hips. Essentially, you want to form a box at first. Slowly walk both hands forward about a hand's length and curl your toes.

- Take in a deep breath and exhale slowly. As you exhale move your backside toward your heels, keeping your arms stretched out ahead and making sure your elbows do not touch the floor.

- Gently lower your forehead, allowing your head to hang loosely in a relaxed way. Maintain a subtle curve in your lower back and press your hands forward, stretching your arms out fully. Pull your hips back to counter the forward motion and to increase the stretching of your muscles.

- Hold this pose for about half a minute, feeling your spine extend in both directions as you do so. Lower your backside to your heels to release from the position and relax the stretch.

Fortunately, this pose can be done by just about anyone. However, if you have knee injuries or issues you should check with a professional first. As stated before this pose is ideal as a restful pose in a yoga workout or it can be used on its own to help release physical and mental tension at any time of day. Additionally, since this pose requires no special environment or equipment it can be done virtually anywhere. The Sanskrit name for this pose is Uttana Shishosana. This is a level 1 yoga pose.

Cobra Pose

The Cobra Pose is another stereotypical pose that just about anyone who has seen anything to do with yoga will recognize. Done properly this pose will have you on the floor, face down, with your legs flat on the floor while you press your torso upward, creating a crescent shape curve from the back of your head to the base of your feet. Needless to say, flexibility is the key concept of this pose. The more flexible you are, the better you will be at performing the Cobra Pose. Alternatively, the more you practice this pose is the more flexible you will become. In the event that you are very stiff, you can opt to perform this pose standing up using a chair as a prop. As you develop flexibility you can progress to performing the pose on the floor as per regular instructions. Benefits of the Cobra Pose include relief of stress and fatigue, relief of sciatica symptoms, firming of the buttocks, strengthening of the spine, stretching and strengthening of the lungs, chest, abdomen and shoulders and an overall increase in flexibility. The steps for performing the Cobra Pose are as follows:

- Lay down on the floor in a prone position. Stretch your legs straight back with the tops of your feet resting on the floor. Place your hand's palms down on the floor directly below your shoulders. Pull your elbows in tight to your body.

- Press down on the floor with your feet and thighs.

- Take in a deep breath and begin to lift your chest off the floor by slowly straightening your arms. Lift off as far as you can without raising your lower abdomen off of the floor. Your thighs, legs, and feet should remain firmly against the floor. Narrow your hip bones in order to keep your center pressed against the floor.

- Pull your shoulders back, keeping your ribs relaxed, to increase the arch of your back. Don't push your ribs out as this will make your back more rigid.

- Maintain this position for about 30 seconds, making sure to take a few deep breaths as you do. Be sure to exhale as you release from this pose and relax back to the prone position.

While this pose is pretty safe to perform there are a few considerations worth noting. If you have any back injury you should avoid this pose. Carpal tunnel syndrome, pregnancy, and headaches can also make this pose dangerous, so avoid it in these circumstances. The Sanskrit name for this pose is Bhujangasana. This is a level 1 yoga pose.

Chair Pose

Unfortunately, despite the relaxed sound of the name, the Chair Pose is not one of the more relaxing yoga poses! This pose is designed to strengthen your legs, abdomen, arms, and feet. When done properly, this pose will have you looking as though you are sitting in a chair with your torso leaning forward and your arms extended straight above your head following the angle of your torso. Beginners can perform this pose with their back against the wall as this will enable them to maintain the pose more easily. Benefits of the Chair Pose include stretching and strengthening of the chest and shoulders, strengthening of the spine, ankles, calves, and thighs, strengthening of the arches of your feet and invigorating the organs in the abdomen as well as the diaphragm and heart. Steps for performing the Chair Pose are as follows:

- Stand on the floor with your feet together and your arms gently bent forward with your palms facing forward. Take in a deep breath and raise your arms over your head so that they are perpendicular to the floor. You can keep your hands apart or you can choose to bring your palms together, keeping your arms straight in either case.

- Breathe out slowly, bending your knees and lowering yourself to where your thighs are parallel to the floor. Keep your knees in front of your feet as this will help you to stay balanced. Additionally, angle your torso forward so that it is over your thighs, creating a low center of gravity. Your torso and thighs should create a 90-degree angle.

- Pull your shoulder blades toward your back and stretch your tailbone downward toward the floor, lengthening your back.

- Maintain this pose for about half a minute, breathing deeply as you do. To release from this pose exhale slowly and gently straighten your knees, lifting through your arms and pulling your arms down to your sides. This motion should be as though you are pulling yourself up by a non-existent handle.

While this pose is more complex than the relaxation poses, it is still pretty safe and straightforward. Again, beginners can choose to practice this pose with their back against a wall as this will help with balance. Performing this pose with a partner will help to ensure that you get the proper alignment for this pose. You should avoid this pose in the event that you are suffering from a headache or low blood pressure. Insomnia sufferers should also avoid the Chair Pose. The Sanskrit name for this pose is Utkatasana. This is a level 1 yoga pose.

Cat Pose

The Cat Pose is another relaxation yoga pose, that is ideal for relieving stress and anxiety. Fortunately, this pose is very easy to perform. Done properly, this pose will have you on all fours with a gentle downward arch in your back. Your thighs will be perpendicular to the floor, going straight up from the knees. Your hands and arms will be directly below your shoulders and your head will be relaxed, facing down as though you are looking at your knees. Benefits of the Cat Pose include stretching and strengthening the muscles in your neck and torso and massaging your spine and the organs in your belly. Steps for performing the Cat Pose are as follows:

- Get on all fours, making sure to be on a mat in order to prevent discomfort to your knees. Position your knees so that they form a straight line between your hips and the floor. Position your wrists so that they form a straight line with your elbows and shoulders perpendicular to the floor. At this point, your head should be straight so that you are looking straight down at the floor.

- Take a deep breath and slowly exhale, raising your spine toward the ceiling. Keep your knees and shoulders firmly in place. This will create a gentle rounding of the spine. Drop your head toward the floor, allowing it to relax. Do not pull your chin to your chest, instead allow your head to hang naturally.

- Take in a deep breath and return your spine to a straight position.

This pose can be repeated as many times as you wish as it is a relaxation pose and does not actually place any strain on muscles or joints. In the event that you have neck injuries or issues, you should simply keep your neck straight while performing the Cat Pose. Otherwise, there are no restrictions on this pose. Beginners can perform this pose with a partner who can assist in getting the curve in the spine right. The Sanskrit name of the Cat Pose is Marjaryasana. This is a level 1 yoga pose.

Gate Pose

For those of you who want a more challenging pose, there is the Gate Pose. This position is designed to stretch out and strengthen the muscles in the sides of your body. These muscles are often untouched by standard yoga poses and regular exercises, so they can be less developed as a result. The Gate Pose targets these otherwise neglected muscles and gets them strong and healthy. When you perform the Gate Pose properly you will be on one knee with your calf stretched out straight behind you. Your other leg will be outstretched straight to the side, creating a 45-degree angle from your hip to the floor, with your foot flat on the floor pointing straight along the line of your leg. Your torso will be curved over the outstretched leg with your inner arm braced against the leg while your outer arm stretches over your head in the direction of your outstretched leg, creating a sideways crescent. Your head will be turned so that you are looking upward toward your stretching arm. The benefits of the Gate Pose include proper and healthy stretching of the spine and torso, stretching and strengthening of the hamstrings, stimulation of lungs and abdominal organs and an opening of the shoulder blades. Steps for performing the Gate Pose are as follows:

- Begin by kneeling on the floor. Stretch your left leg straight out to your left and press the bottom of your left foot flat to the floor. Keep your right knee in a straight line below your right hip and form a straight line between your left foot and your right knee. Rotate your pelvis slightly to the left, angling your upper torso slightly to the right. Make sure that your left knee is pointing upward.

- Take in a deep breath and raise your arms so that they are pointing out sideways and parallel to the floor. Bend your torso to the left, laying your left hand on your left shin. Ultimately, your hand should stretch down as far as possible, hitting your ankle or even the floor, but the shin is a good place to start. Position your right hand on your right hip and push your pelvis downward toward the floor. Bring your hand up to lift the lower right ribs, thereby creating a little space between the ribs and the waistline.

- Take in a deep breath and bring your right arm over the back of your right ear. Bend your torso further pushing through your arm to do so. Only go as far as what feels comfortable. Do not strain yourself and do not 'bounce' in this position.

- Maintain this position for between half a minute and a full minute. Make sure that you straighten out on the inhale, bringing yourself out of the position gradually and gently. This position can be repeated a few times, and of course, it should be reversed in order to provide equal benefits to both sides of your body.

While the Gate Pose is still considered a level 1 pose it is a little more strenuous than some of the more relaxing poses, so greater care should be taken while performing it. Anyone with serious back or knee injuries or issues should consult a professional before attempting this pose. Additionally, beginners or persons with physical restrictions should begin by performing this pose with a partner, preferably a trained yoga instructor. The Sanskrit name of this pose is Parighasana. This is a level 1 yoga pose.

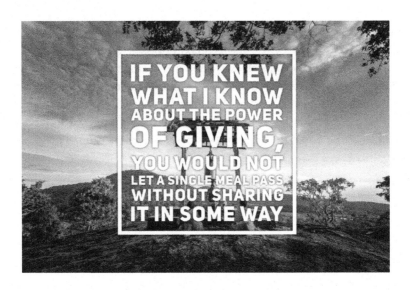

CHAPTER 10

BUDDHISM IN OUR TIME

"If you knew what I know about the power of giving, you would not let a single meal pass without sharing it in some way."

– *The Buddha*

The Age of Information – our time – is when the world and the people in it are in an interconnected state. Every day, there are more discoveries in science and technology that seek to answer life's questions and solve many problems. People use the internet to access a limitless amount of data on practically any topic their mind could think of. It has also enabled one to create communities despite staying in one spot and to converse with anyone from any part of the world.

Yet, as the people in our time continue to surge through increasingly complex discoveries and innovations, one question remains the same: how much do we really know about ourselves? Are we slaves to desires and self-centeredness? On the other hand, are we still capable of upholding such timeless virtues as generosity and kindness?

Such reflections have led many towards the path that the First Buddha took over two thousand years ago. However, Buddhism in our time, including its principles, culture, and rituals, is not only tolerant but actually adjusts to the needs of those who seek it. This is what makes it so relevant and pragmatic in modern society.

In this chapter, we will talk about the possible reasons why Buddhism is still accepted in our modern society.

Buddhism as a Moral and Intellectual Compass

The concept of *karma* details how your choices regarding thoughts, words, and actions influence you and everything around you. However, Buddha's teachings do not just stop there. Rather, they show you how you can become more mindful of this responsibility so that you can lead a purposeful and truly happy life.

The best part is the teachings of the Buddha do not just let you figure things out for yourself. Instead, it provides you with the Four Noble Truths to help you reflect deeply on what causes your suffering, and with the Noble Eightfold Path to enable you to solve such a problem. When you have that compass to follow, you have a huge amount of information that can help you to find your direction in life. The Noble Eight Fold Path is simple for people to understand as the basis for living their lives. Although much has changed since the time of the original Buddha, taking note of the Noble Eight Fold Path and studying how it relates to your life helps you to become more in tune with yourself. Your meditation practice helps you to not only understand your own reactions to life, but it also helps you to understand the self-discipline used in Buddhism to stay within the path given by the original Buddha.

Buddhism as a Lifestyle

Another reason why modern man has openly accepted the teachings and practices of the Buddha is how it positively influences one's way of life. Buddhist concepts such as the Five Precepts, Meditation, and Mindfulness make so much sense to the modern mind, even if one does not acknowledge spirituality.

The ability to exercise free will when it comes to heeding the Buddha's advice adds to the appeal of this ancient discipline in the modern world. Unlike much of the world's dogmas, Buddhism places emphasis on one's volition and encourages one to put experience before accepting the Dharma.

There are plenty of other ways to view the role of Buddhism in our time. Through learning and experiencing it, you too can construct your own perspective of it. Now, you might want to ask yourself, "Why am I drawn to Buddhism? Which part of its practices and teachings are relevant to my life in modern society?" You might be surprised by what you can reflect on by giving yourself some time to answer these questions.

When you learn how to meditate, you also learn how to be in the breath. This means learning deeper breathing techniques that help you to remain focused in the now. Mindfulness uses all of the senses to be in the moment, rather than avoiding it by letting the mind drift to the past or future and thus lose the opportunity to enjoy the now. The breathing techniques also have a value from a health point of view since most human beings use very little of the lung capacity when they breathe. When you learn to breathe in the way that is used during meditation, you enable your bodily functions to work better because the sympathetic nervous system – which is responsible for many functions in your body – is then able to distribute the oxygen around your body.

You are also taught the importance of posture and that's where yoga comes in very useful as this is one of the first lessons learned. The posture of the body helps in the process of meditation because you are taught by gurus or teachers to position yourself in such a way that the energy centers of the body are able to receive the freedom needed to feel all of the joy that Buddhism is able to impart. Blocked energy paths, otherwise known as Chakras, need to enable energy to pass through them and these are located along the length of the spine, this meaning that posture is vital to the flow of energy. If you have never thought of this, it may be worthwhile looking at a chart of the Chakras to understand their significance and yoga teachers will make you conversant with these chakras and their uses when you go through yoga class.

They help your energy to flow correctly, but they have other functions as well. For example, when you meditate, the idea is to try and open the third eye or see things that you would not normally see. This includes the use of intuition and intuitive thought. Other chakras are

108

located along the spine in the neck, heart, navel, and base of the spine as well as the crown chakra, located at the top of the head. The movements and the breathing exercises that you are introduced to during yoga exercises help to keep these channels open and they have great significance to your levels of concentration and your ability to meditate.

Buddhists today learn all about the significance of the process of meditation and the discipline entailed. In a material world, it's very hard for people to go through the process of learning, though those who do come to a better understanding of life through their studies. Learning from gurus or yoga teachers, Buddhists go through the different processes of breathing and meditation for the purpose of reaching that higher state that comes with practice of the Nobel Eight Fold Path.

In our time, people have developed the habit of worrying and of being anxious and the figures produced by health authorities show that medical experts and looking for alternatives to traditional medicines to help with what is a seeming epidemic. Many hospitals and medical facilities in Europe are no introducing patients to mindfulness classes in an attempt to help to stem the suffering without the use of long-term medication. In fact, there are books written by the Dalai Lama in conjunction with medical experts who compare the values of the Buddhist to those of people who do not practice Buddhism and are interested in the way that the philosophy can be used to help alleviate the suffering of people in today's world. The results so far have been astounding and more and more people are turning toward the Buddhist philosophy, even without initially understanding of what that meant to their everyday lives. By taking up meditation and yoga classes, they are having values instilled that lead them to further exploration of the Buddhist way of life.

Buddhist centers across Europe and the United States are today making inroads in introducing students to the Nobel Eight Fold Path in conjunction with mindfulness and meditation classes. Having attended centers in Europe, the approach to Buddhism is open all and Buddhists are very welcoming to those seeking answers to their questions. The training that is done within Buddhist centers in France and in the United Kingdom encourages the study of the philosophy hand in hand with teaching students the benefits of each of the paths taken when one chooses to use the philosophy as a way of life.

109

CHAPTER 10 B

BUDDHISM AS THE 'TOTAL PACKAGE'

Buddhism as philosophy and metaphysical

CHAPTER 11

THE PRACTICES
OF BUDDHISM

"Resolutely train yourself to attain peace."

— The Buddha

Throughout the centuries, the practices of Buddhism have been transforming based on the people who continue to uphold them. In fact, how the practices are adopted is based on the culture of different societies.

Yet, one thing remains the same, and it is that the core values of Buddhism are preserved. After all, such virtues are being strong-willed, generous, kind, and selfless are not only universally accepted, but also timeless.

In this chapter, you will learn about the general Buddhist practices. You will learn how they can help you to become stress- and anxiety-free at the least, and how they can help you stay motivated as you follow the Noble Eightfold Path.

Mindfulness Meditation

When you talk about Buddhism, you cannot avoid mentioning the concept of meditation. It is the core of the practice. Additionally, scientific studies can attest to its mental and physical benefits. Meditation is a generally accepted and widely recommended way to reduce stress in everyday life, improve cognitive and emotional intelligence, and increase positive thinking.

Much can be said about the different types of Mindfulness Meditation. While some are discussed in detail in Chapter 18, you can conduct further research on your own on the following practices:

Theravada Buddhism Meditation:

- Anapanasati
- Satipatthana
- Metta
- Kammatthana
- Samatha
- Vipassana
- Mahasati
- Dhammakaya

Vajrayana and Tibetan Buddhism Meditation

- Ngondro
- Tonglen
- Phowa
- Chod
- Mahamudra
- Dzogchen
- The Four Immeasurables
- Tantra

Zen Buddhism Meditation

- Shikantaza (sitting meditation)
- Zazen
- Koan
- Suizen

Chanting and Mantras

Another common practice in Buddhism is chanting. Buddhist monks in different parts of East and Southeast Asia practice chanting on a regular basis to help them improve their concentration as well as reflect deeply on Buddhist concepts.

Buddhists modernists use phrases in their spoken language to create mantras that help them sink deeper into their meditative state as well.

You may be familiar with the "Om," which is a sacred mantra that Buddhists chant at the start of all mantras. According to ancient Hindu texts, Om is the one eternal sound that exists in the past, present, and future. It embodies the birth, life, and death, and it is used and heard every day. Interestingly, it is said that by chanting "Om," the vibrations it causes helps relax the body and mind.

There are also centers whose gurus give individual chants to students based upon the year the time and place of birth and these are personal to the student.

Chanting is found useful in many ways because it allows the student to concentrate on a given thing rather than allowing the mind to wander. Although this was not the specific purpose of mantras, it does help to cut out unnecessary thought processes which help the student to meditate more successfully. It also helps the student with breathing, since some mantras are used in rhythm with the breathing and help the student to deep breathe and to chant the mantra on the outward breath.

Vegetarian or Vegan Lifestyle

While it must be noted that the First Buddha himself never mentioned anything against the consumption of meat, many Buddhists choose to live the vegetarian or vegan lifestyle.

One of the main reasons for this is the cardinal principle of harmlessness, or *ahimsa,* which states that all living beings have within them the divine spiritual energy. Therefore, by harming another being one is harming the self as well.

Some Buddhists who choose to eat meat do so only out of necessity. For instance, those who live in cold climates can only survive if on a diet that is rich in fat and protein. In such cases, the Buddhists would then choose only the meat of ethically raised animals. In other words, the animals lived a full and relatively happy and free life and were slaughtered in the most humane and painless manner for their meat.

Ultimately, the decision to choose your diet rests in your hands as the Buddha himself explained. Of course, no one is exempted from the karmic results of eating meat, especially if the living being was slaughtered specifically for you. This is worthy of note since Buddhist monks are often given food and there is a story about a Buddhist monk who was extremely hungry. He was given a plate of chicken and was looking forward to eating it until he was told that the chicken had been slaughtered specifically for him. In this case, he was not permitted to eat it since this goes against Buddhist belief and he was considered the cause of the killing.

As you can see, many – if not all – of the practices of Buddhism can easily be incorporated into the modern lifestyle. It is up to you on how you perceive and practice these rituals each day. After all, it is only through experience that you can truly witness the benefits of these practices.

A DISCIPLINED MIND BRINGS HAPPINESS

CHAPTER 12

HOW TO PRACTICE THE FIVE PRECEPTS OF BUDDHISM

"A disciplined mind brings happiness."

– The Buddha

The Five Precepts of Buddhism are the fundamental ethical guidelines for Buddhists. However, they are not to be regarded as a rigid set of rules, but as gentle suggestions on how to live a life free from suffering. After all, the Buddha always emphasizes the being's power of choice.

Below is a description of the Five Precepts as well as suggestions on how to put each of them into practice:

The First Precept: Do not intentionally kill any Living Being.

"I undertake the precept to refrain from killing."

The followers of the teachings of Buddha should not entertain the idea of causing harm or, worse, killing any other living beings, whether human or animal. Instead, they cultivate genuine concern for and loving-kindness towards the welfare of others.

You can bring the First Precept to mind each time you are tempted to hurt a living being, be it an insect or another person. The least you can do is to avoid having anything to do with the senseless killing of animals, such as for sport or for overconsumption. It is this First Precept, in fact, that has inspired many Buddhists to become vegan.

The Second Precept: Take only what is given to you.

"I undertake the precept to refrain from taking what is not given."

This precept greatly discourages stealing and "borrowing" items from others without returning them. By following this precept, Buddhists seek equality in the distribution of resources and, at the same time, they wish to instill the value of generosity in themselves.

To put the Second Precept into practice in the modern world, you can work towards living within your means and paying off debts that you owe. Many Buddhists have turned to the minimalist lifestyle because it guides people to let go of consumerism and live meaningful lives. In this day and age, this is also a common practice because the simplicity of this precept is that it gives so much back. The common saying that "less is more" really comes into its own when you examine how it applies to modern day living. In the consumerist society that we live in, we have to realize that the material wealth of the world is little in comparison with the spiritual wealth and therefore, the need to have or to own things takes a back seat to being happy with what we have in life.

The Third Precept: Do not misuse the senses.

"I undertake the precept to abstain from sexual misconduct."

In the traditional sense, the third precept advises against letting one's sexual drive dominate one's life, as it is understood that it leads to suffering. Instead, Buddhists are encouraged to live a contented life with thoughts and actions that serve a meaningful purpose.

However, you may interpret the Third Precept as something that encompasses all abuse of the senses. For instance, it can be taken as advice against overeating, which leads to many sufferings, such as obesity. Instead, the Buddhist is guided towards doing things (including the consumption of food) in moderation and with good purpose.

Misuse of the senses can include an excess of anything that causes suffering. Excess drug consumption, excess smoking or indeed any excess at all that touches the senses is considered to be against this precept.

The Fourth Precept: Do not speak of falsehood.

"I undertake the precept to refrain from false speech."

The Buddha teaches that one should not lie, slander, and engage in malicious gossip. Instead, one should only speak words of truth and kindness and be motivated by positive intentions when engaging in a conversation with others.

It can be tempting at times to talk negatively about something. However, now that you have learned of this Precept, perhaps you can practice mindfulness in the way you speak. If you find it hard to hold yourself back from saying things that could hurt others, you might want to consider keeping a journal. This is a great way to begin acknowledging and monitoring your thoughts before you turn them into spoken words. The thing that is hard for people to accept is that hurtful things that you say to people come back to you and hurt you as much as those to whom the words were directed. By being true to yourself and kind to others, you suffer less and you are able to feel better about who you are. Your journal is simply a means to record your negativity so that you don't make the same mistake again.

The Fifth Precept: Avoid Intoxicants.

"I undertake the precept to refrain from taking substances that cause a lack of attentiveness."

The Fifth Precept places emphasis on the harm caused by drinking alcohol and taking unnecessary stimulants and drugs. Buddhists are on the path towards improving their concentration and cultivating rational thought, therefore, this precept is a gentle reminder of what causes the opposite of these.

As you can see, each of the Five Precepts makes perfect sense. However, following them rests solely on your own volition, especially since the Buddha encourages everyone to think and experience things for themselves rather than to follow through blind faith. The Five Precepts are fairly easy and logical for people to follow and help to put mindfulness in place in your life. Note them down in short form so that you are reminded of them and can correct your behavior when you find yourself being pulled away from them by life in general. Your awareness of these Precepts makes you more responsible for your actions and by taking these seriously, you lessen your own suffering and also take control of how your mind is able to perceive mindfulness.

ALL CONDITIONED THINGS ARE IMPERMANENT – WHEN ONE SEES THIS WITH WISDOM, ONE TURNS AWAY FROM SUFFERING

CHAPTER 13

THE ESSENCE OF LIFE
AND ENLIGHTENMENT

*"All conditioned things are impermanent – when one
sees this with wisdom, one turns away from suffering."*

– The Buddha

When a human being has satisfied his basic needs – food, water, shelter, security, and so on – he begins to wonder about the purpose of existence or the essence of life. The Buddha himself had reflected on this especially as he may have been a noble whose basic needs were fully satisfied.

After attaining Enlightenment, the Buddha then began sharing his reflections with others. His teachings were then compiled into what is now the Dharma, and its purpose is to help those who are searching for the essence of their own lives and ultimately attain Enlightenment.

Of course, this does not mean everyone should live life in the exact same way. Rather, it means reaching your own unique highest potential in the same way the Buddha did when he attained Enlightenment.

So how do you begin your path towards self-actualization? According to Buddhist teachings, you can find it by helping others, by cultivating the Four Divine Abodes, and by applying the Six Perfections in your life.

Helping Others

Compassion is the humane quality of understanding the suffering of other sentient beings and the inclination towards helping them through it. Buddhism teaches compassion because it enables one to value life in general. The Buddha himself chose to help guide others towards the path of Enlightenment because of compassion.

To find essence in life in this aspect, you may begin taking on a sense of responsibility for other beings, especially those who are in a more difficult position than you are. Perhaps you can volunteer for a local charity organization or use your skills for the welfare of others.

Cultivating the Four Divine Abodes

Meditation is the recommended way to cultivate the Four Divine Abodes, namely:

- Loving-kindness,
- Compassion,
- Sympathetic bliss, and
- Equanimity

To do that, here are the steps that you can take. Keep in mind that you can always adjust this method to suit your preferences based on your experience of it:

1. In a quiet and peaceful place, spend some time reflecting on any one of the Four Divine Abodes.

   For instance, if you are going to meditate on Loving-kindness, reflect on how to describe this feeling. Try to embrace this as part of who you are and by meditating on them, you will find that your meditation has real purpose and that you come closer to understanding what enlightenment is.

2. Visualize a person in your life who can easily make you genuinely feel this quality.

   If you are meditating on loving-kindness, you might be thinking of a loved one whom you care for with all your heart. Often, these are the people who bring out the best in us. You can see through their actions and their belief in you what it's like to incorporate these qualities into your life.

3. As you invoke the feeling of the quality, let it reverberate from within you to your surroundings.

   In the case of loving-kindness, you can visualize not just your loved ones but also other people whom you do not usually care for in real life. Through practice, you could even direct it towards those whom you do not particularly like. The point of this is that you overcome your prejudices and make yourself capable of shutting off prejudice and being able to see beyond it.

4. Continue to extend the feeling of the quality towards all beings in the world. Visualize it pouring from your heart towards them.

   You can constantly practice this form of meditation so that the Four Divine Abodes will eventually become more natural to you. Embracing these qualities will then enable you to see the true essence of life. This helps you to become more optimistic. It helps you to increase your mindfulness and your energy levels so that the energy that you give off is positive and helps those people around you to see joy and happiness in their own lives.

Applying the Six Perfections

The Six Perfections (paramita) consisted of the path of the Bodhisattva. It was designed to combine compassion with discernment into the true essence of life. They are:

- Generosity,
- Moral behavior,
- Patience,
- Effort,
- Concentration, and
- Wisdom

Let us take a look at the practical steps you can take to instill the Six Perfections in your life:

Generosity

To be generous means to be open towards helping others without expecting anything in return. There are several ways to become more generous to others, but in traditional Buddhist teachings, there are four ways:

1. To share the teachings of the Buddha

   Leading others towards a path that frees them from suffering is a generous thing to do. It enables others to think and act for themselves and to gain the right motivation to living a truly meaningful life. This isn't as hard as you may think it is. When you experience the positivity of your belief in the philosophy of Buddhism, you are able to impart that to others and to share with them the joy that this brings to your life. Each person must choose their own route through life. You cannot choose it for them. However, you can influence those you care about so that they learn the generosity of spirit that comes from knowing you. Give without expectation of thanks or return. When you do, you feel nearer to the spiritual awakening than you do when you add strings to the things that you give.

2. To protect other beings

   Every day, other living beings, humans, and animals alike, have to live through life-threatening conditions. The only way for them to be saved is by the help of those who are in better positions than they are. You can be generous with your time and efforts to help protect them and lead them to a better life. In day to day life, this could mean giving to the poor or being generous with your time when people are sick and in need of company. There are many ways that you can give your protection to others and it's quite possible that you already do this with your family. Extend your protection to people around you who are less well off than you.

3. To inspire and motivate others

   One of the best ways you can help others is by motivating them to have the courage to pursue a better life. You can also practice what you teach through meditation and follow the teachings of the Buddha. When others see that you are capable of it, they too might be inspired to do the same. Inspiration does not involve any expectation. You can share what you know and discuss the teachings of Buddhism, but you cannot influence people to follow the way simply because you say so. They need to see your example and to be inspired by it, rather than being expected to follow a way that is not seemingly natural to them.

4. Offering material goods

Living beings need food, shelter, clothing, and other materials to improve their quality of life. Your generosity in the form of such gifts can tremendously benefit them. In fact, this way is easily most associated with the concept of generosity. In the Protestant and Catholic religions, people give alms. These are collections of money that are used for the benefit of the church or of other people. When you have things that you no longer need, there are always those who have less than you. Offering them the things you know will make their lives more comfortable should become a natural way forward for those who believe in Buddhist philosophy.

Moral Behavior

Moral behavior is exercising self-discipline so that you do not cause harm to other beings. The effort placed into choosing the more difficult but morally upright path instead of the easy but wrong one is one of the ways to uphold this Perfection. Another is to cultivate genuine compassion for others through prayer, meditation, and good work.

Through constant practice, moral behavior will become more natural and spontaneous to you.

Patience

The more you practice the teachings of the Buddha, the more naturally patient you will be. Being patient actually protects yourself and others, because it restrains you from allowing feelings such as ill will and anger to transform into destructive actions. As your patience continues to grow, you will notice that such negative feelings become weaker until you can no longer feel them.

To help you develop patience, here are traditional Buddhist practices to try:

1. Acknowledge and Accept Suffering

   Life is peppered with positive and negative experiences, making suffering an inevitable part of life. However, by accepting this reality, you develop the patience to go through these negative experiences. Through this, you do not become overwhelmed by feelings of regret, resentment, or anger associated with these events in your life. The acceptance of the Four Noble Truths will help you with this. The very first Noble Truth tells you that suffering is something that happens in life. However, when you strengthen your ability to accept suffering, you are stronger when such an event happens that causes that suffering.

2. Stay calm

   Staying calm in spite of frustrating or dangerous events actually leads to good karmic results. At first, it might be a challenge to stay calm when someone is attacking you. However, by taking a step back, you are able to analyze the best steps you can take based on the situation before you react. The more you practice, the easier it will be for you to stay calm and be mindful before you speak and act or even react.

3. Develop patience in pursuit

   As you continue to practice the teachings of the Buddha, there will be times when your old habits resurface and tempt you to steer from the path. However, you must remain patient in your efforts even if you do not always see immediate results. To do that, simply draw yourself back by reminding yourself of the teachings that have led you to start your journey in the first place. You will find that meditation and mindfulness will help you with your patience levels. You will be less inclined to make hasty decisions and thus more capable of looking at problems from a global scale, rather than the narrow focus that small-mindedness encourages. Since you are naturally more generous with people, you will find you are naturally more generous with your time and understanding.

Effort

Effort in this sense refers to one's commitment and perseverance in choosing to do what is right. It also means doing things with enthusiasm instead of feeling as if you are abstaining and resisting from something. Some Buddhist teachers even emphasize that effort is the foundation of the other Perfections because, with it, the rest would naturally fall into place.

To practice Effort, you must understand and acknowledge the presence of the three obstacles that impede it. These are defeatism, trivial pursuits, and laziness.

Defeatism is entertaining negative, self-defeating thoughts, such as thinking that you do not have what it takes or letting your fears overcome you. You can overcome this through mantras, or affirmations that remind you that you have the ability to be committed and perseverant if you so try.

Trivial pursuits are the activities that distract you and keep you from achieving your full potential. They serve no meaningful purpose in your life other than to grant you momentary and superficial desires. While there is nothing wrong with relaxing and engaging in them occasionally, you should work against becoming addicted to them.

Laziness is simply choosing not to do something because you do not want to. You can think of it as a merger between the first two obstacles because your negative mindset towards the task causes you to engage in trivial pursuits instead, a common phenomenon known as procrastination.

The only way to get out of it is by having the energy to just do the task right away. Of course, it would be easier to do that if you equip yourself with good physical and mental health and by applying the right strategies, such as starting the morning right.

Concentration

Meditation is the key to improving your concentration, so take the time to practice it each day. Start with simple meditation exercises, such as sitting and breathing meditations. Then, once you become accustomed to them, you can move on to deeper levels, such as those that enable you to reduce physical pain and emotional trauma. To sit and meditate, you can choose to use a seated stance on a cushion on the floor where your legs are bent at the knees and crossed at the ankles. It is hard for people who are new to meditation to take up the more traditional lotus position at first, and this position, provided your back is straight is a good position for meditation. Your hands can be cupped with your palms facing upward and your thumbs touching. If you do use a cushion for meditation, it's a good idea to sway from left to right and back again to ensure that your body is grounded and comfortable before starting on the breathing exercises. When you start to meditate, make sure that you are in a space that is not busy or which is free from distractions.

Close your eyes to help the process. Then breathe in through the nostrils deeply until you feel the air filling the upper gut. Imagine the air going into your body. Many Buddhists use a counting system at first, but later find that they no longer need to use it because their bodies become accustomed to the rhythm of breathing and do not need the count. The ideal count is 8 for the inhalation, and 10 for the exhalation. While meditating, the only thoughts that you should experience are those of this moment and the process of breathing. Detach yourself from the world and your troubles and when thoughts come into your mind, learn to let go because this is not the moment, although don't make a huge deal of it because it is natural for the mind to process thoughts.

You will find that early morning meditation will help your concentration levels during the day and that this, in turn, will help you to have the energy to get through the difficulties that life presents to you. Meditation is a daily event and should be as much a part of your everyday life as breathing.

Wisdom

The highest level of the Perfections, Wisdom is the ability to discern one's own thoughts to choose what is right for the welfare of others and yourself. According to Buddhism, the Perfection of Wisdom means being able to see reality for the way it is and not shrouded by your own judgments.

As always, the best advice to follow so that you can cultivate Wisdom is by following the teachings of the Buddha. However, if you wish to know how to begin, you can start by determining your habitual thought patterns. One important thought habit you should identify is how you would normally view yourself, other beings, and your surroundings. Then, if you notice that your thoughts, words, and actions are being directed by your own misconstrued perceptions, you can do something about it.

Now, you might be wondering how you can find the essence of life and enlightenment through helping others, the Four Divine Abodes, and the Six Perfections. Well, the best way to find out is to go out there and practice them. After that, you can then reflect on answering such questions once again.

Keeping a diary at the end of daily meditation helps you to be able to see your progress. In fact, it serves another purpose too. When you have finished meditation, your heartbeat will be slower than usual and your blood pressure will be reduced. Taking notes in your diary of your progression and thoughts upon what you can do next time you meditate to help the process gives your body the time to transition back to the normal heartbeat and blood pressure before rising to begin your day. Think of it as your record of the progress that you have made with your meditation and concentration practice.

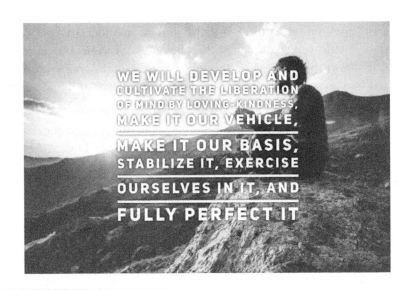

WE WILL DEVELOP AND
CULTIVATE THE LIBERATION
OF MIND BY LOVING-KINDNESS,
MAKE IT OUR VEHICLE,

MAKE IT OUR BASIS,
STABILIZE IT, EXERCISE

OURSELVES IN IT, AND

FULLY PERFECT IT

CHAPTER 14

THE TREASURES
OF BUDDHISM

*"We will develop and cultivate the liberation of mind by l
oving-kindness, make it our vehicle, make it our basis, stabilize it,
exercise ourselves in it, and fully perfect it."*

— *The Buddha*

The Three Treasures, also known as the "Three Jewels," are the
cornerstones of Buddhism. They are the Buddha, the Dharma, and the
Sangha. When aspirants seek to become Buddhists, which is by
accepting the teachings and seeking to practice them, traditionally they
would declare the following:

"I take refuge in the Buddha, I take refuge in the Dharma, I
take refuge in the Sangha."

In other words, whenever they find themselves lost in the midst of the
mundane world, they can always find their way back with the help of
the Three Treasures.

Now, let us take a look at each of the Three Treasures.

The Buddha

The Buddha is the First of the Three Treasures. Take care not to interpret the meaning of the phrase "I take refuge in the Buddha" as seeking the protection and benevolence of a god. Rather, it means that you are opening your mind to the path that will lead you to become a Buddha.

Taking refuge in the Buddha means you are acknowledging the possibility of becoming like Buddha, and to be instilled with the mindset that can lead to the attainment of Enlightenment. The Buddha that you see on the altar of Buddhist Temples is not a God. He is an inspiration for all those who seek to become Buddha themselves. Nowadays, in the western world, there are many representations of Buddha that you can use yourself in your meditation space to help you to be inspired when you step into your practice of mindfulness and meditation.

The Dharma

The Second Treasure is the Dharma, and it is the teachings of the Buddha. The Four Noble Truths serve as the foundation of this Treasure. By "taking refuge in the Dharma," you acknowledge the value of learning the Four Noble Truths and practicing the Noble Eightfold Path. It's a good idea to regularly read the text of the Noble Eightfold Path and keeping this in short form note format, you are easily reminded of what is expected of you when you follow the route that was created for your sense of happiness by the original Buddha.

The Sangha

The Sangha is the community of Buddhists. In the traditional Theravada teachings, it is composed only of the monastery. However, among Mahayanists and Buddhist modernists, it encompasses all who follow the same path, that which is pointed by the Buddha. A Buddhist can find and give guidance to fellow Buddhists by coming together to learn and practice. The Buddha recognizes the value of interacting with those on the same path, therefore, the Sangha is recognized as the Third Treasure. If you want to seek the guidance of those who are already Buddhas, then a Temple may be able to give you this guidance.

Similarly, a guru may be able to answer questions that you may have about the teachings and there are Buddhist centers all over the world which serve as communities for those seeking out the teachings of the original Buddha.

Now that you know of the Three Treasures, would you agree that finding refuge in them enables you to stay on the path towards Enlightenment? Only you can tell, for your experiences are always the best testament to this tenet.

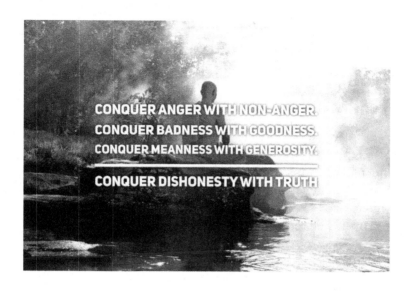

CONQUER ANGER WITH NON-ANGER.
CONQUER BADNESS WITH GOODNESS.
CONQUER MEANNESS WITH GENEROSITY.

CONQUER DISHONESTY WITH TRUTH

CHAPTER 15

THE POISONS
OF BUDDHISM

*"Conquer anger with non-anger. Conquer badness with goodness. Conquer
meanness with generosity. Conquer dishonesty with the truth."*

– The Buddha

In Chapter 2, you learned about the Three Fires of Buddhism, which
also happened to be called the Poisons. As was mentioned, these three
are the inner character flaws present in all sentient beings. They are the
very reason why Desire and Suffering (dukkha) exists, and the first step
to getting rid of them is to acknowledge their existence.

In this chapter, let us take a closer look at each of the Three Poisons:
Moha, Raga, and Dvesha.

Moha or Delusion

The Buddhist concept of *moha* can be translated to delusion, dullness, or
confusion. A being's ignorance can be traced to this root. According to

traditional Mahayanists, it is the reason for a being's destructive thoughts and actions. In the Wheel of Life, moha is represented by the boar.

The cure for Moha lies in Wisdom or *prajna*.

Raga or Greed

The Sanskrit word *raga* literally translates to "color" or "hue," but it is used to represent the qualities of greed, lust, desire, and sensual attachment. All forms of craving, particularly those sensual and sexual in nature, fall under this poison. Any being who seeks and finds excitement over worldly pleasures that can be felt by the senses are afflicted by it. The rooster is the symbol for raga in the Wheel of life.

The cure for Raga can be found in Generosity or *dana*.

Dvesha or Ill Will

The term *dvesha* is Sanskrit, and it means "hate" or "aversion." It is represented by the snake in the Wheel of Life. Harboring dvesha towards anything, including other beings and yourself, leads to suffering.

One can be cured of Dvesha through Loving-kindness, or metta.

If you take a look at an image of the Wheel of Life, you will see at the center the Three Poisons as their animal representations. Specifically, you will notice that the snake and the rooster are coming out from the mouth of the boar. This means that the first poison – delusion – is the source of the latter two poisons – greed and ill will.

However, what is a delusion? It is the mindset attached to a false sense of self and reality. To help you recognize the presence of the first poison, here is a famous Buddhist story:

> Close your eyes and visualize that you are outside walking in the evening, lamp in hand. The moon is hidden in the clouds, but the stars are out and are enough to guide you as you follow the path that is familiar to you. Then, ahead of you, you see something.
>
> It is long and coiled, and it appears as if it is ready to strike out at you. You feel a sense of panic as your body is suddenly frozen with fear. Then, the clouds moved, allowing the moonlight to shine on this coil and you realized...it is merely a piece of rope.

Just to be on the safe side, though, you decide to move your lamp around you to check whether there really is a snake around. After doing so, you realize that there was no snake in the area in the first place. It was just the idea of the possibility that struck you. Your mind relaxes, and your heart drops back to its normal rate as you continue to follow the path.

After reading this analogy, what do you think the "snake" represents? If you think that it represents your false sense of self, then you are right. But as long as you hold on to the idea that that piece of rope was a snake, then you will continue to feel fear, stress, sadness, disappointment – suffering. However, through wisdom as symbolized by the moonlight, and if you make the effort to look around, then you will discover that this false sense of self does not really exist.

Therefore, the cure to the Three Poisons is to acknowledge that your concept of who you are or should be are false. Once you let go of this, you can move towards cultivating wisdom, generosity, and loving-kindness.

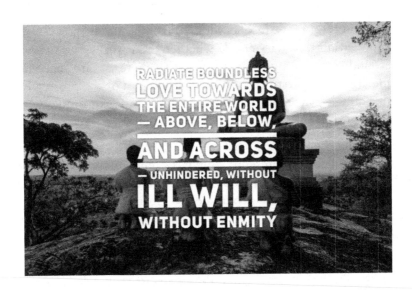

RADIATE BOUNDLESS
LOVE TOWARDS
THE ENTIRE WORLD
— ABOVE, BELOW,
AND ACROSS
— UNHINDERED, WITHOUT
ILL WILL,
WITHOUT ENMITY

CHAPTER 16

PRACTICING MINDFULNESS MEDITATION FOR STRESS AND ANXIETY RELIEF

"Radiate boundless love towards the entire world — above, below, and across — unhindered, without ill will, without enmity."

– The Buddha

Suffering is an inevitable part of life and, until you have reached the state of Enlightenment, it helps to know how to cope with each challenge you face. Stressful situations can stir feelings of pain and anxiety, moreso if they have to do with the things that you are most attached to. The good news is, Buddhist teachings can show you ways to cope with such emotions and events. The most effective of these is through Mindfulness Meditation.

Mindfulness is the trait of paying close attention to the present moment. It helps you take a step back from your worries about the future and fears of the past. It allows you to see the reality for what it is, unclouded by assumptions and expectations. Studies show how effective mindfulness meditation is in reducing stress both instantaneously and over the long term. This chapter will show you how to apply this Buddhist practice for stress and anxiety relief.

Stress is a natural reaction to situations that you perceive as threats. It triggers you to either face the problem or flee from it. However, the mind is incapable of differentiating between the stress caused by a life-threatening scenario (such as a house on fire), or by one that is not (such as a looming deadline). In both cases, the body and mind react in the same way.

The interesting thing about stress is that it is triggered only by how you *perceive* the source. Do you still remember the Snake and the Rope analogy in Chapter 15? Therefore, if we apply Buddhist teachings for stress relief, here are the steps that you can take:

Acknowledge the physical and mental symptoms of stress or anxiety.

How can you tell whether you are stressed out or anxious? What makes you realize that it is what you are experiencing, not some other state?

Some people notice that their heart beats much faster, or that they experience cold sweats. Others strangely start to smile or even laugh uncontrollably, while others blank out or stutter. Yet, others start to churn out all sorts of negative thoughts that plague them for the rest of the day.

Be mindful of the symptoms you personally experience when you are stressed or anxious.

Observe how often you experience stress and what triggers it.

Keep a small notepad or create a file on your phone to keep track of the moments where you feel most stressed or anxious each day. You can recall and take note of them by the end of each day. Doing so will help you become more cognizant of these stressful experiences. It will also enable you to pinpoint the sources of your stress.

For instance, take note of the time of day when you felt stressed out, its intensity based on a scale (such as between 1 and 10), and the situation, person, thing, or even thought that triggered it.

Aside from that, you can also take note of how you reacted to the situation. Did you flee the scene? Did you just stand there and do nothing? Whatever it is, note it down.

Consider the Best Ways to Respond to Stress and Anxiety

The body responds to how the mind perceives a stressful situation, so the best way to feel less stress is by calming the mind first. Therefore, the stronger your mind is, the more resistant your body would also be towards stressful situations. Begin by recognizing your power to choose.

For instance, you can use your journal to reflect on how you normally responded to these situations. What do you think would be the better ways to handle them? There are actually plenty of healthy options. Here are some that are in line with the principles of Buddhism:

- Practice breathing meditation to regularize heart rate and breathing. You will find that this is covered in detail within the pages of this book.
- Go on a walking mindfulness meditation to temporarily step away from the stressful situation and allow your mind to think deeply.
- Stay away from intoxicating substances that will only impede your judgment (particularly alcohol).
- Exercise with mindfulness to train the body to be more resistant.
- Detach yourself from the situation as if you are a mere spectator.
- Chant a mantra that helps strengthen your mind, such as "everything is going to be alright," or "I am calm and collected."

Once you have come up with positive responses to stress and anxiety, you can then practice them regularly through meditation.

Breathing Meditation

Mindful breathing in and of itself is simply being aware of your breath without changing it. Practicing it is a great way to not only acknowledge and express gratitude for the ability to breathe but also help you regulate it during stressful situations.

Breathing meditation, on the other hand, can be done using a variety of techniques. One is the deep breathing meditation, which is incredibly effective at reducing stress and anxiety. Here are the steps to do it:

1. Sit or lie down comfortably. Keep your back straight and shoulders relaxed. You can choose whether to use a hard chair and keep your feet planted flat on the floor or whether you want to use a cushion, bend your knees and cross your ankles. Your hands need to be posed one cupped by the other with the palms facing upward and your thumbs touching each other.

2. Focus on your natural breath, noticing each movement of the body as the air passes through from your nostrils to the upper abdomen.

3. Place one hand on your chest and the other on your belly as you continue to breathe naturally. This will help you to feel the air entering your body and creating a pivot motion which will tell you that you are breathing sufficiently deeply.

4. Begin breathing deeply. As you inhale, notice how your belly rises, but not your chest. As you exhale, notice how your belly falls while the chest remains relatively still. As you breathe, this movement should form a rhythm.

5. Continue to breathe deeply for a few minutes until you feel more relaxed.

Another breathing meditation to try for stress and anxiety relief is by counting your breaths. This helps you to relax and calm the mind as well as the body. Here are the steps. After a while of meditating in this manner, you may not need to count but will know instinctively the length of your breaths by the rhythm they form in the movement of your stomach.

1. Sit or lie down comfortably; shoulders relaxed and back straight. Your clothing should be comfortable.

2. Begin breathing naturally. Then, when you are ready, start counting each breath. Inhale first, then exhale, counting both as one. The length of the breaths can also be counted if you wish to. The ideal is 8 for the inhale and 10 for the exhale. Then count your one, two or whatever number you are on.

3. Count each breath up to ten. As soon as you reach that number, begin counting your breaths from one to ten again. You will find

that this is a little difficult at first because thoughts wander into your head.

4. If your train of thought gets lost along the way, simply begin counting at one. Take care not to be critical towards yourself for losing track. Neither should you be critical for allowing thoughts to enter your head. Just be aware of them and then dismiss them, but do not feel any animosity toward yourself for having thought those thoughts.

5. Continue to count your breaths until you feel more relaxed. You must always remember after you meditate to let your body get up slowly because your heart rate and your blood pressure will slow down. This helps you to feel more balanced and happy inside yourself.

Mindfulness in walking meditation

I have included this aspect of meditation because it is useful to use when you are away from home and are faced with stressful situations. You may find yourself having to meet with people who cause you stress or having to face a meeting that worries you. Walking meditation will help you to overcome the fear and strengthen your mind with purpose so that you will be clear-headed and able to face whatever that fear is with a calmness.

1. Loosen any clothing that may be restrictive.

2. Find a quiet place where you can walk. A natural environment where you can breathe fresh air is always going to be the preferred area for this exercise.

3. Stand with your back straight and start to take steps, with your head slightly lowered, watching each movement of your feet.

4. Breathe in and move the foot forward being aware of the movement of all the muscles of the foot.

5. Feel your other foot lift off the ground and move forward, being conscious of the movement of the muscles in the leg, the knee and the calf.

6. Be conscious of the foot touching the ground and continue to breathe in and out using your nostrils for the inhalation and feeling the air go through to your lower chest area.

7. When you breathe out, move your leg in time with the breath so

that you are always in rhythm with your breathing.

8. Think of nothing else at all. If thoughts happen, let them slide away into the background and go back to your concentration on walking and meditating.

This kind of meditation helps you to alleviate the types of stressors which are brought about by events in life. Interviews, meeting new people or going to a meeting can all be precursors to this kind of stress and this type of meditation can help you to keep your composure and control what you are feeling inside of yourself. Be in the moment. Be in the steps that you take. Breathe.

Be Mindful of your Thought Patterns

Modern-day stressors are not the main cause of your stress and anxiety. It has more to do with your perspectives. The teachings of the Buddha offer plenty of ways to transform your thought patterns for the better.

However, anyone can get distracted from these because of the demands of daily life. Thus, to help draw your mind back towards focusing on Buddhist teachings, here are ways to help you be more mindful of the way you think and perceive yourself and your surroundings:

See things from a different angle.

Imagine yourself in someone else's shoes, such as someone whom you admire (perhaps the Buddha himself?). How do you think this person would perceive the situation? How would he respond to the source of stress? Sometimes this exercise can really change how you see things yourself. You may have already done this on your normal day to day life. I remember as a child thinking that I was a concert pianist when I had piano practice and it's almost the same thing, except that you are using that other person as your focal point and looking at the situation from the angle that person would see it, rather than seeing it as yourself. This helps you to avoid distraction and to use inspiration to guide you.

Identify the individual parts of the stressor.

Seeing a big issue as a whole can be taxing, emotionally and mentally. Therefore, it would be a good idea to break the issue down into smaller, more manageable parts so that you can stop procrastinating and start solving it. It may hurt you to think about the things that stress you initially, but when you can identify them and can dissect the problem into smaller portions, it makes it easier to cope with. The reason that we put off dealing with stressors is because in themselves, they cause us stress and we believe in avoidance. However, if you dissect the problems, they become smaller and more manageable and you can gradually expose yourself to these stressors so that they don't cause the same psychological damage. Let me give you an instance. If you have problems with relationships, write down the problems in list format and work on one of them at a time until they become less of a problem. If you are stressed by going into a public place, try entering a place where you are more aware of who is likely to be there and gradually spread your wings a little and include new people into your circle, so that you are not so anxious with strangers.

Consult an expert.

If you acknowledge the fact that you alone are incapable of solving your stress and anxiety problem, then do not be afraid to approach an expert. Receiving guidance from someone who has already gained the wisdom to solve such problems will not only benefit you greatly but also enable you to solve the problem for yourself later on in life. The way that the subconscious mind works when you have stressors is that it responds to them in the way that your mind has taught it to respond. You can change this programming by mild exposure to the trigger and gradually by realizing that you can respond in a positive way to whatever that trigger is. Professionals help people to do this if you are afraid of doing it on your own.

Keep in mind that stress and anxiety are merely the signals your mind and body send to let you know that a deeper problem lies with you. It is up to you to uncover it as you continue to move forward on your spiritual journey. As you uncover those stressors and understand why you react in the way that you do, you are able to see quite logically that the stress factor is less when you decide when that stressor is introduced. Therefore, by exposing yourself to those stressors in controlled circumstances, you can reprogram your thoughts so that you are able to switch off the negative connotations that you associate with those stressors and take control of your life.

Be open to relearning and letting go of certain things in your life.

However, if you do stumble, just pick yourself up, brush yourself off, and move on. There is no deadline or competition towards Enlightenment. Remember that the Buddha himself said that all beings are equally capable of reaching it.

The Buddhist philosophy will help you to come to terms with whatever you perceive as your own personal weaknesses and help you to strengthen your resolve against the things that give you problems. If these repeat themselves and cause the stress to return, go back through this book to find out which areas of your life need to be strengthened because as you learn to incorporate the Nobel Eight Fold Path into your life, the problems of this world become less and you are more capable of embracing life to its fullest.

CHAPTER 16 B

ADDITIONAL FORMS
OF MEDITATION

There are various meditation techniques that can be used by anyone at any time and virtually in any place. These techniques can help to center your thoughts, thereby helping to eliminate the veritable monkey mind that otherwise has our thoughts random and scattered. Alternatively, certain meditation techniques can help to reduce stress, depression, anger and any other extreme emotional condition that would create or increase the physical suffering you experience. While there are almost countless variations of meditation available, they all fall into three basic forms—concentrative, open awareness and mindfulness. These three meditation techniques, when practiced on a daily or fairly regular basis, have been shown to improve a person's health both in terms of physical wellbeing and in terms of mental wellbeing. Needless to say, these techniques can require some practice before you are able to get the full benefits they have to offer. However, they are actually quite simple and straightforward in nature. Therefore, if you are able to set aside the time each and every day, and you have a relatively quiet place where you can practice, then you can put any or all of these techniques to use in your life.

Concentrative Meditation

Concentrative meditation is perhaps the form that most people envision when they hear the word 'meditation'. The primary characteristic of this form is that the practitioner focuses on a single item, thereby eliminating all other thoughts from their mind. In this scenario, a person sits in a comfortable position, usually cross-legged, and they focus on a single object. This object can be just about anything imaginable, however, the objects most commonly used include candles, plants, colors, water features, and crystals. As the practitioner sits in their comfortable spot they will observe their object of choice, allowing that object to fill their mind. One by one they let go of any thoughts that are currently in their minds until eventually, the only thing that they are thinking about is the object they are observing. Normally this process takes from 10 minutes to 20 minutes, depending on the time the practitioner has available and the amount of practice they have in meditating. It is advised that a beginner practice this form of meditation in 10-minute durations, as longer durations can cause the practitioner's mind to begin to wander. As the individual becomes proficient they can extend the length of each session accordingly. The basic technique of this meditation is as follows:

- Find a quiet place where you can be undisturbed for at least ten minutes.

- Find a comfortable place to sit. It is usually recommended that you sit on the floor, so be sure to bring a pillow, mat or some similar item that will make the floor more comfortable to sit on. In the event that you cannot sit on the floor for physical reasons, you can sit in a chair or on a sofa. The important thing is to not allow yourself to drift off to sleep if you have to sit on a sofa!

- Place the object you have chosen as your focal point in front of you. It is ideal if you have a table to set it on as this will create a natural line of sight.

- Begin to breathe deeply, concentrating on the depth and regularity of your breathing until you feel physically relaxed and mentally calm.

- Start to focus on your meditation object, forcing your mind to fixate on the object and to let go of any other thought or emotion you are experiencing.

- Remain focused on your object, maintaining a deep, steady breathing rhythm. Whenever a thought or emotion pops up that is unrelated to your object simply increase your focus on the object and allow that thought or emotion to fade away.

In addition to visual objects, sounds can be used in concentrative meditation. This is where the form of meditation known as Transcendental Meditation comes into play. Transcendental Meditation is the form where a person sits in a comfortable position, just as already described, and chants a mantra. This mantra can be as simple as a single sound or word, or it can be as complex as a whole thought or sentence. In the case of a single word or sound, the objective is for the practitioner to become completely fixated on the sound, much the same way that they would be with an object in the previous example. One of the advantages of using sound as opposed to using an object is the vibration that the sound produces. Many traditions teach that vibration can actually purify the energy of a person, bringing it to a higher or better frequency. Different sounds can be used to obtain different results, and this is where it is beneficial to have a teacher or guide to refer to. A trained meditation expert will be able to advise you on which sound would benefit you the most. Variables such as mood, body type, personality type and other similar considerations can make certain sounds more effective than others. Full sentence mantras can be used to create a focused thought process, similar to that created by a visual object. Using an affirmation as a mantra will help to focus your mind on the thing you want to achieve the most, thereby helping to establish right thinking, right speech, and even right action. The steps of this meditation are as follows:

- Choose a quiet place where you can be alone for the period of your meditation practice.

- Find a comfortable place to sit, preferably on the floor. Again, be sure to bring a mat or pillow so as to prevent discomfort while sitting. Additionally, a chair or other seating area can be used if necessary.

- Begin to breathe deeply, focusing on the length and regularity of your breathing. Once your breathing is relaxed and natural and your body and mind are also relaxed you can begin to recite your mantra.

- Recite your mantra in a way that is relaxed and consistent with your breathing. Be sure to be calm in reciting your mantra as you want the sound of the words to be soothing.

- Focus on your mantra until all other thoughts and emotions are gone from your mind. Whenever a thought comes into your mind, increase your concentration on the sound of your mantra until it fades away again.

144

Open Awareness Meditation

Another form of meditation that is very effective is what is called Open Awareness Meditation. The goal of this form is virtually the opposite of the goal of Concentrative Meditation. While the practitioner of Concentrative Meditation focuses on an object until that object is the only thing that occupies their mind, the practitioner of Open Awareness Meditation strives to not focus on any single thing. Instead, Open Awareness Meditation encourages the practitioner to allow their mind to freely roam from one thing to another, never fixating on one object or situation for more than a few seconds. The goal of this form of meditation is to instill the practitioner with a sense of detachment from their surrounding environment. If Concentrative Meditation is about taking a few steps closer to physical reality, Open Awareness is about taking several steps back. Since attachment to things is considered a significant cause of suffering, then Open Awareness Meditation can be highly beneficial in eliminating suffering by training the practitioner to become mentally and emotionally detached from their surroundings.

At first, this form of meditation may seem a bit hard to understand. After all, how can letting your mind wander from one thing to another ever be a good thing? The truth of the matter is that many people perform this type of meditation on a daily basis without ever realizing what they are doing. Any time you sit outside when you go to a restaurant, and you watch the people walking by while you eat, you are performing Open Awareness Meditation. People watching, crowd watching, and any other practice that allows a person to observe things from a detached perspective is nothing less than a form of Open Awareness Meditation. Therefore, if people watching is something that you have already done in the past, then this is a form of meditation that will come easily and naturally to you. The steps of Open Awareness Meditation are as follows:

- Find a place where you can comfortably watch an active environment for the specified amount of time. Like with Concentrative Meditation, a period between 10-20 minutes is ideal.

- Sit in a comfortable position. Unlike Concentrative Meditation, a chair or other conventional seating arrangement is ideal for this form.

- Begin to breathe deeply and regularly. Focus on your breathing until it becomes relaxed and natural. You should also maintain this focus until your body and mind feel more relaxed.

- Begin to observe your surroundings. In the event that you are sitting outside a café, you can begin to watch the people walking by. Purposely observe a single person for a span of about 5-10 seconds, and then turn your attention to someone else.

- Repeat this step for the duration of your time. People-watching outside is an ideal environment for this meditation as most of the people won't be in your field of view for more than a few seconds.

- It is important to actually focus on the person, taking in one or two details, before moving on to the next. If you don't take in any details then your mind will begin to wander and the exercise will produce no results.

- In the event that a person you are paying attention to stops walking, be sure to not fixate on them for longer than the 5-10 second span. If you fixate on a person or event then you become attached to that thing. Therefore, it is critical to constantly shift your attention from one person or event to another.

Another environment where Open Awareness Meditation can be performed easily is in a social event, such as a concert, a play or a sporting event. While you will not necessarily be able to leave after the 10-20 minutes that you meditate that is not a problem. In this situation, you will simply take your attention away from the event itself and begin to observe other elements around you. If you are at a sporting event you can begin to notice the field on which the game is being played. Observe the color of the grass, the lines on the field, and even the goal posts, or whatever other equipment or fixtures there are. Next, you can begin to observe other spectators, much the same way that you would observe people walking by at a café. As you begin to become aware of the other people around you your mind will become detached from the event itself. This is a wonderful way to practice detachment, especially if the event is something you are particularly interested in. After all, being able to take your concentration off of an important soccer match is no small feat! Simple steps to follow for this technique are as follows:

- Assuming you are at a match or event, begin to pay attention to your breathing. Begin to take in deep, regular breaths and focus on your breathing until your breaths are relaxed and natural.

- Stay focused on your breathing until your mind and body also feel more relaxed.

- Once you have achieved relaxed breathing begin to look around at the people around you. Do not pay attention to the event itself, instead, pay attention to those who are paying attention to the event. In this way, you go from being an observer to observing the observers themselves. This is the basic principle of being in a constant state of detachment.

- Shift your attention from one person or object to another every 5-10 seconds. Be sure to note details of each thing you observe before moving on to the next.

- Keep this up for 10-20 minutes. When you are done, then you can go back to enjoying the game!

Mindfulness Meditation

One form of Mindfulness Meditation has already been covered in this book, however, this form is somewhat different. This particular style of Mindfulness Meditation serves to combine the elements of Concentrative Meditation and Open Awareness Meditation. So far the forms of meditation listed have provided the practitioner with two very important skill sets. In the case of Concentrative Meditation, a person develops the skill of concentration, much as the name suggests. This helps to eliminate the monkey mind mentality that plagues the vast majority of people most of the time. Confusion, poor memory, scattered thoughts and the like are the result of the proverbial monkey mind. And these are the very things that lend to so much suffering on a daily basis. By developing focus and concentration a person can eliminate the monkey mind and all of the harmful effects that it brings. In the case of Open Awareness Meditation, a person develops the skill of becoming detached from their surroundings. Since the attachment is another cause of suffering, then this is another vital tool in the quest for Nirvana. Only when a person is able to be clear-headed and emotionally detached can the fires of suffering be truly extinguished. Mindfulness Meditation is the practice of merging both of these skills into a single master-skill, the skill of transcendent living.

The way that this variation of Mindfulness Meditation works is that it combines focus and detachment. This meditation can be performed absolutely anywhere, including at home, at work, or anywhere in between. Since this form of meditation will require the most practice before you are able to do it effectively it is probably best that you start practicing it at home. This will allow you to focus more easily, while also providing a calmer environment to meditate in. The trick to mindfulness meditation is to focus on a single activity and then to take the same mental step back that you did in the case of Open Awareness Meditation. By doing this you are able to be focused while also being detached. The huge advantage of this meditation is that it will allow you to develop the Buddha Mind while living your day to day life. You won't have to find the quiet time or a quiet place to perform this meditation. Rather, this is a form of meditation that you can perform no matter where you are and no matter what else you are doing.

The ideal way to begin practicing this meditation is to perform it while you are doing household chores. Any household chore will give you the focus point you need for the concentrative element, provided that it is a chore that will take at least 10 minutes to perform. That said, washing dishes is a perfect chore for Mindfulness Meditation. The first thing you will want to do is to actually begin performing the chore, in this case washing the dishes. Once you begin washing dishes focus on your breathing, just like in all other meditative techniques. Next, you will want to focus on the act of washing the dishes themselves. While you might feel that you pay attention to washing dishes normally, this will require greater focus. The point of focusing on the dishes now isn't to ensure that you are doing a good job, rather it is to make sure that your mind is clear of all thoughts and feelings not associated with washing dishes.

Once you have achieved total focus on washing the dishes, then you go to the second phase of the meditation—the open awareness phase. At this point, you should shift your attention from washing dishes to the other things going on around you. Pay attention to any people in the vicinity, being sure to only focus on each person for no more than 5-10 seconds at a time. Again, it is important to take in a few details while focusing on a person before moving on to the next point of focus. Keep shifting your attention from one thing to another until you achieve the state of being the observer. Now you are an active observer, both participating and observing. It is at this point that you should achieve a feeling of being present yet detached from the environment you are in. This technique will take some practice to perfect as there are multiple skills being applied at once. Additionally, the opportunity to lose focus is increased in this scenario as you are actively performing a task while not necessarily being alone. Even so, that is the whole point of this method. This form of meditation is designed to help you take your learned skills of concentration and detachment and to be able to apply them in the regular world. The basic steps of this meditation are as follows:

- Find a chore that needs to be done that will take at least 10 minutes to do. While washing dishes was used as the example above it is not the only chore available. Folding clothes, sweeping a floor, vacuuming, washing a car or any other such activity will do as well. Any chore that involves machinery should be avoided, such as mowing a lawn, as any lapse in concentration could increase the risk of serious injury. Keep it simple and keep it safe!

- Begin to perform your chore as you normally would.

- Begin to focus on your breathing, taking in deep, regular breaths. Stay focused on your breathing until your breathing becomes natural and relaxed. Additionally, stay focused on your breathing until your body and mind reach a more relaxed state.

- Next, begin to focus on the chore you are performing. Focus on the chore the way you would on a candle or other object using the Concentrative Meditation techniques.

- Stay focused on the object until all unrelated thoughts and feelings in your mind fade away.

- Once you have achieved a clear mind begin to shift your attention to other things using the techniques of Open Awareness Meditation.

- Focus on each object or person for no more than 5-10 seconds, being sure to take in details of each thing you pay attention to.

- Keep doing this until you feel detached from your environment. You want to feel as though you are an observer with no attachments to anything or anyone around you.

- Maintain this practice for at least 10 minutes. As you get better at the technique you can increase your time as much as you want. The ultimate goal is to be able to perform this technique anywhere, anytime.

The one thing that separates the Mindfulness Meditation technique from the Concentrative and Open Awareness techniques is that you will be able to perform it even when you are actively involved in life. The more that you practice Mindfulness Meditation while doing regular things is the better you will become. Eventually, you will find that the meditation will evolve into an actual way of life. Instead of intentionally performing Mindfulness Meditation you will begin to practice it out of habit. After a while, it will change your whole way of life as it will redefine your state of mind. With this, a serious reduction in stress, anxiety, anger, and any other detrimental mindset will follow. Before long you will begin to live a life of focus and detachment which will lead you ever closer to the state of Nirvana that frees you from all human suffering.

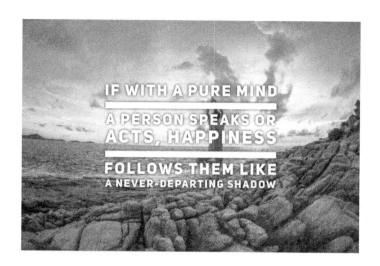

IF WITH A PURE MIND
A PERSON SPEAKS OR
ACTS, HAPPINESS
FOLLOWS THEM LIKE
A NEVER-DEPARTING SHADOW

CHAPTER 17

THE TEACHINGS
OF BUDDHA

*"If with a pure mind a person speaks or acts, happiness
follows them like a never-departing shadow."*

— The Buddha

Ever since the first Buddha, or Shiva, began teaching, followers of the
Buddhist practice had studied his words. These words are meant to
educate you, not only on reaching enlightenment but on how to live
each day with empathy and love. Many times, Buddha's teachings were
created in the form of stories that gave a lesson or taught amoral.
Buddha's words are wise and hold relevance in any time period in
history. Though some of the teachings are blanketed slightly in
misogynistic viewpoints, modern-day Buddhism has bent to the new
place of women and children in the world. You will also find many of
the words of Buddha are used in chants and in prayer as it is believed
that repetition of his teachings will further open up the unconscious
mind. It is a good idea if you choose to lead a Buddhist lifestyle that

you acquire the Dhammapada and study his words very carefully. In these words, you will find the wisdom to lead you closer to a full and complete Enlightenment. This chapter is dedicated solely to various excerpts from the teaching of Buddha.

Excerpt from The "Dhammapada

Hatreds never cease by hatreds in this world. By love alone they cease. This is an ancient Law. (5)

A fool who thinks that he is a fool is for that very reason a wise man. The fool who thinks that he is wise is called a fool indeed. (63)

Though he should conquer a thousand men in the battlefield a thousand times, yet he, indeed, who would conquer himself is the noblest victor. (103)

Hard is birth as man, Hard is the life of mortals, Hard is the hearing of the Sublime Truth, Hard is the appearance of a Buddha. (182)

Not to do any evil, to cultivate good, to purify one's mind, - This is the advice of the Buddhas. (183)

There are no sons for protection, neither father nor even kinsmen; for him who is overcome by death, no protection is there from kinsmen. (288)

The Last Teaching of the Buddha

1. Beneath the Sala trees at Kusinagara, in his last words to his disciples, the Buddha said:

   "Make of yourself a light. Rely upon yourself: do not depend on anyone else. Make my teachings your light. Rely upon them: do not depend upon any other teaching.

   Consider your body: Think of its impurity. Knowing that both its pain and its delight are alike causes of suffering, how can you indulge in its desires? Consider your 'self'? Are they not all aggregates that sooner or later will break apart and be scattered? Do not be confused by the universality of suffering, but follow my teaching, even after my death, and you will be rid of the pain. Do this and you will indeed be my disciples."

2. "My disciples, the teachings that I have given you are never to be forgotten or abandoned. They are always to be treasured, they

152

are to be thought about, they are to be practiced. If you follow these teachings you will always be happy.

"The point of the teachings is to control your own mind. Keep your mind from greed, and you will keep your behavior right, your mind pure, and your words faithful. By always thinking about the transience of your life, you will be able to resist greed and anger and will be able to avoid all evils.

"If you find your mind tempted and so entangled in greed, you must suppress and control the temptation; be the master of your own mind.

"A man's mind may have made him a Buddha, or it may make him a beast. Misled by error, one becomes a demon; enlightened, one becomes a Buddha. Therefore, control your mind and do not let it deviate from the right path."

3. "You should respect each other, follow my teachings, and refrain from disputes; you should not, like water and oil, repel each other, but should, like milk and water, mingle together.

"Study together, learn together, practice my teachings together. Do not waste your mind and time in idleness and quarreling. Enjoy the blossoms of Enlightenment in their season and harvest the fruit of the right path.

"The teachings which I have given you, I gained by following the path myself. You should follow these teachings and conform to their spirit on every occasion.

"If you neglect them, it means that you have never really met me. It means that you are from me, even if you are actually with me; but if you accept and practice my teachings, then you are very near to me, even though you are far away."

4. "My disciples, my end is approaching, our parting is near, but do not lament. Life is ever changing; none can escape the dissolution of the body. This I am now to show my own death, my body falling apart like a dilapidated cart.

"Do not vainly lament, but realize that nothing is permanent and learn from it the emptiness of human life. Do not cherish the unworthy desire that the changeable might become unchanging.

153

"The demon of worldly desires is always seeking chances to deceive the mind. If a viper lives in your room and you wish to have a peaceful sleep, you must first chase it out.

"You must break the bonds of worldly passions and drive them away as you would a viper. You must positively protect your own mind."

5. "My disciples, my last moment has come, but do not forget that death is only the end of the physical body. The body was born from parents and was nourished by food; just as inevitable are sickness and death.

"But the true Buddha is not a human body: - it is Enlightenment. A human body must die, but the Wisdom of Enlightenment will exist forever in the truth of the Dharma, and in the practice of the Dharma. He who sees merely my body does not truly see me. Only he who accepts my teaching truly sees me.

"After my death, the Dharma shall be your teacher. Follow the Dharma and you will be true to me.

"During the last forty-five years of my life, I have withheld nothing from my teachings. There is no secret teaching, no hidden meaning; everything has been taught openly and clearly. My dear disciples, this is the end. In a moment, I shall be passing into Nirvana. This is my instruction."

In Service

1. There are seven teachings which lead a country to prosperity: First, people should assemble often to discuss political affairs, and to provide for national defense.

Second, the people of all social classes should meet together in unity to discuss their national affairs.

Third, people should respect old customs and not change them unreasonably, and they should also observe the rules of ceremony and maintain justice.

Fourth, they should recognize the differences of sex and seniority, and maintain the purity of families and communities.

Fifth, they should be filial to their parents and faithful to their teachers and elders.

Sixth, they should honor the ancestors' shrines and keep up the annual rites.

Seventh, they should esteem public morality, honor virtuous conduct, listen to honorable teachers, and make offerings to them.

If a country follows these teachings well, it will surely prosper and will be held in respect by all other countries.

Misfortunes

"It is wrong to think that misfortunes come from the east or from the west; they originate within one's own mind. Therefore, it is foolish to guard against misfortunes from the external world and leave the inner mind uncontrolled. "

Enlightenment

Enlightenment has no definite form or nature by which it can manifest itself; so, in Enlightenment itself, there is nothing to be enlightened.

Enlightenment exists solely because of delusion and ignorance; if they disappear, so will Enlightenment. And the opposite is true also: there is no Enlightenment apart from delusion and ignorance; no delusion and ignorance apart from Enlightenment.

Therefore, be on guard against thinking of Enlightenment as a "thing" to be grasped at, lest it, too, should become an obstruction. When the mind that was, in darkness becomes enlightened, it passes away, and with its passing, the thing which we call Enlightenment passes also.

As long as people desire Enlightenment and grasp at it, it means that delusion is still with them; therefore, those who are following the way to Enlightenment must not grasp at it, and if they reach Enlightenment they must not linger in it.

When people attain Enlightenment in this sense, it means that everything is Enlightenment itself as it is; therefore, people should follow the path to Enlightenment until in their thoughts, worldly passions, and Enlightenment become identical as they are.

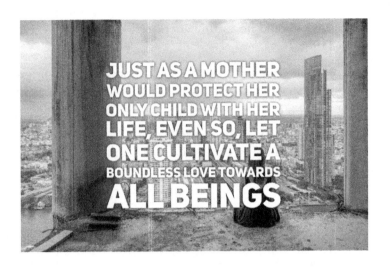

JUST AS A MOTHER WOULD PROTECT HER ONLY CHILD WITH HER LIFE, EVEN SO, LET ONE CULTIVATE A BOUNDLESS LOVE TOWARDS ALL BEINGS

CHAPTER 18

CREATING A MEDITATION SPACE IN YOUR HOME

"Just as a mother would protect her only child with her life, even so, let one cultivate a boundless love towards all beings."

— *The Buddha*

For those that live in areas of the world where Buddhist temples are prevalent, creating a personal meditation space is not as important. However, for those in the Western World where finding a temple can be nearly impossible, having a place in your home to practice is vital. Even if you choose not to subscribe fully to the path of Enlightenment, meditation can have an enormous effect on everything in your life. Through meditation, you learn to control your mind, dig deeper into your unconscious mind, and soothe your body from the anxiety-ridden world outside your doors.

There are many different things to run over before creating your meditation space. You don't want to just plop a pillow in the middle of the living room and attempt to find inner meditative calmness, especially for those who don't live alone. Your space should be sacred to you and only used when looking for deep meditation. It doesn't have to be its own room, but it should be a space that is left undisturbed by others. By understanding what you need to create this sacred space you will be able to do so wherever you go, whether it is in your home, a friend's home, or in a hotel when away for vacation or business. The following section will take a look at the things you should look at when creating your meditation space.

Understand Your Intentions

Not everyone that creates a meditation space is looking to submerge themselves in the life of a Buddhist completely. In fact, some simply want a space they can quietly sit and reflect on the moment. Your space for meditation and reflection is going to be specific to your needs, so you need to take the time to decide what your intentions are. If they are for deep meditation then picking a space in your home where you are going to find peace and quiet is important. You may even find that being close to nature helps you with this quest. Thus, if you have an area of the garden where you can cut yourself off from the noise and bustle of life this will be a good space for your meditation.

Whatever the reason, behind your want for a meditation space, realize and accept that the everyday world is riddled with things that keep you from practicing mindfulness and awareness. From the television, the computer, and even your phone, there are technologies all around us that prohibit our true self from receiving the attention and exercise it needs to become aware of the truth around you. Understanding your intentions will help you begin deciding on exactly what type of space you are going to need to create.

Locate That Space

Once you understand what your intentions are, you will know what type of space in your home, you are looking for. You don't need to have an entire room dedicated to a meditation space, though if that is something that is possible for you, go for it! However, a corner of a room where you know the activities of that space fit perfectly with your intentions is exactly what you are looking for. Remember to find a space that, when not in use, will not be disturbed by the actions, people, and pets in your home. There is nothing more distracting than cat hair floating up from your meditation pillow when you sit in stillness.

For those that are more experienced in the art of meditation, you can also think of an outdoor space that you can use in any weather condition. For example, in my home, we have three dogs and a kid, so my meditation space is under the covered part of the deck in front of my Buddha statue. I do live in the mountains so during the cold winters I choose a space in my bedroom to create a meditation area. Your meditation space needs to accord with your circumstances. One particular friend who meditates on a regular basis has chosen a space in the open, high in the hills where she is able to get close to nature and to feel that oneness that she so believes to be part of her sanctity. Her explanation is useful perhaps to those who may find similar spaces. "When you are in that space that is truly an inspiration, you get to recognize how small you are and that's the beginning. Being small and humble is part and parcel of Buddhism and you also feel that the world around you inspires you to be the very best that you can be, regardless of how small nature makes you feel. Being small is not negative. Each pebble on the beach has its place."

This choice is very personal to what helps you truly relax. The sounds of nature and the warmth of the sun is the place that I find myself most at peace, but you may live in a city where the honking of horns and the sounds of people could be incredibly distracting. Buddhist temples across the world are located in every different facet of society from calm and quiet mountain tops to strip malls in the city. The point of it is, when you walk through those doors and into that space, you find calmness disconnected from the chaos of the world around you.

Décor

This is your personal space, and you can decorate it in any manner you wish. Most take a minimalistic approach in order to avoid distractions, but you can decorate your area in any way you want. Think about the things that bring you the most comfort and relaxation and try to incorporate those into your space. If you are uncomfortable, your mind will be uncomfortable as well, and you will find that reaching a deep stillness and meditative state will be difficult. Just as finding intentions and deciding upon a space, decorating your meditation area is a hugely personal decision.

My meditation space, outside is simply my Buddha statue and my meditation pillow. The outside nature brings all the décor I need to feel at peace. When I bring it inside, however, it takes a bit more effort to separate the comfort of my home from the pure comfort of a place of peace. I use soft blankets to help calm me, a picture of Buddha because the statue is too large to bring indoors, candles for a calming sense, and incense in a fragrance that invokes spiritual ideas. Your décor may also align with any Buddhist rituals you may decide upon. Oftentimes, your space may change if you observe any holidays associated with Buddhism.

Different things give inspiration to different people. You may find that you have a particular photograph that is inspirational and that's something that you can incorporate into your meditation space as well because sometimes the type of meditation can be focused meditation which means that you meditate with your eyes open but concentrate on a particular object that you find to be inspirational.

However, you decide to decorate your space, make sure that it is comforting, safe, and right for you. This, as you can see, is a common theme in Buddhism since the path to Enlightenment, though often reached through the same routines, is an extremely personal journey that you take. Remember that becoming comfortable in this life is important because even if you do achieve true Enlightenment, you still have to live in this life.

Direction

Depending on the type of meditation you practice, the direction you are facing may affect the outcome of your meditative state. Understand your meditation needs when you choose your space and when you decide the décor. Remember that what you experience before you close your eyes will aid your mind in reaching that relaxed state so that you are able to reach down to your inner self. Those that choose a more relaxing and calm meditation often face themselves North while those who have a more rejuvenating expectation face East or West. These changes are dependent upon the type of Buddhism you practice as well as the intention of your stillness. When I create my space inside, I try to make the entire space as calming as possible so that if I turn my pillow away from my focal point I am still relaxed and at ease. My bedroom, for example, is decorated very simply, and before I begin my meditation, I make sure everything is picked up and somewhat organized. Clutter can create anxiety which sparks the conscious mind and inhibits my stillness.

Items You May Want for Your Space

As mentioned before, your space is a reflection of your own personal comfort and intention. You may have an incredibly spiritual area while you may also have a simple space not related to religious or spiritual ideas at all. These are some of the pieces that you may find useful in your newly created meditation space.

Buddha

Due to the fact that religion is such a pertinent thing in society, we often think of statues or pictures as a worshipping item. However, in Buddhism, as we have said before, there is no ultimate creator that we focus our attention on. Buddha is a teacher and a symbol of mindfulness and intention. Having a visual representation of Enlightenment and the wise teachings of the first Buddha, may help you focus, be reminded of mindfulness, and remember the teachings that these individuals gave in order to help you on your path to Enlightenment.

Candles and Incense

Candles are some of my favorite relaxation items to include in my space. Bright artificial lights often stiffen my minds resolve to let go and allow my inner self to take over. However, complete darkness makes me sleepy, and with such a busy world, meditation sometimes tries to force me to sleep. Candles help me focus my energy, they create an awesome focal point for me, and the shadows that they cast help me when I'm trying to loosen the tension from my physical body. Personally, I use unscented candles as the fragrances are usually too artificial for me, but you can choose any type, color, and size of candle you want. Just make sure you put them in a safe place so that you don't have the concern of accidents on your mind when trying to meditate. Nothing will bring you out of a meditative state quicker than a curtain fire.

Incense is not for everyone, but I have used it all my life when trying to relax. My favorite incense scent is lavender since it helps to calm my nerves and brings peace to my space. Incense also lingers for quite a while, so even when I am not meditating and happen to pass by my room, I get a whiff of lavender and am instantly reminded to remember my intentions for each day, and to be mindful of the world around me. When burning incense make sure to put it in a safe place, and it is recommended to not put it directly in front of you. The smoke that comes from it can be strong, but if it is burning on the other side of the room, you will get that passing fragrance that helps to get your thoughts back on track.

Meditation Pillow

One of the most annoying and distracting things you will notice when practicing meditation is to ignore the discomfort your body tries to use to distract you. Let's face it, it may have been comfortable at ten years old to sit for hours on the floor, but as we get older, that isn't necessarily ideal. From aching backs to numbness of limbs, there are so many things that you can be distracted by. Meditation pillows, especially those specifically made for meditation help to align your body with the correct posture and keep it comfortable during the process.

My personal choice for a meditation pillow includes a large flat pillow and then a small one for under my butt that is filled with beans. The large pillow keeps my ankles from getting sore resting on the ground while the one for sitting on conforms to my body in a way that allows me to sit cross-legged, at an angle. This keeps my back and spine aligned and avoids aching areas while I am trying to focus. In reality, all you really need is your body and a place to sit, and though I have trained myself to be able to meditate anywhere, especially since I travel so often, in my home, I want to make sure I am as free of distractions as possible.

For those who have the inability to sit on a cushion on the floor, there is nothing wrong with using a hard chair. The position for meditation on a chair would be slightly different in that you would use your feet flat on the floor to center your body during meditation. Thus, you need a chair where your back is straight, rather than one that encourages you to recline. The height of the chair should be such that your feet can be placed flat on the floor with no difficulty at all.

Singing Bowl

Singing Bowls are used for various things from meditation and music to rituals and funerals. Singing bowl produces a soothing and calm sound that can help your mind relax into a meditative state. Oftentimes, they are used to signal the beginning and end of a meditation. You can ring a singing bowl and then start your breathing, falling further into meditation, and finding that you don't even hear the sound anymore. Sometimes they can be used simply to realign you and bring a calming energy. A singing bowl of the right pitch can also be used to start your chant. This is a good way to start your meditation session if you use chant, but remember that chanting takes some practice.

Ring the singing bowl and then breathe in. On the outward breath, you tend to sing the Om or your chosen chant and then breathe in again. You may find during the course of meditation that you no longer need the chant, but if this is your way of meditating and you are more comfortable with it, the bowl should be placed near to your place of meditation so that after the initial sound from the bowl, the bowl is replaced beside you as you continue your journey into meditation.

The further you delve into your meditation routine the more you will be aware of what you need in your space to make it the perfect tranquil location. Nature is everywhere and in everything so if your space is inside, inviting pieces of nature such as rocks and plants into your space may help to align you. Soft colors, soft music, and temperature control are also important things to think about when you are entering your space. Once you know what will work for you in your complete space, you will be able to move and bend with that in order to create spaces in other places such as your office, a hotel room, and even when you are on vacation. The most important aspect of all of this is to feel comfortable and intentional in your actions and to enjoy everything around you.

You will find eventually that all of that comfort comes from within you and that you are able to meditate in any space and not be put off by your surroundings. If you want to try something really special that is comforting and wonderfully calming, then I would advise that you choose a spot where you can see a lot of the natural environment and enjoy the warmth of the sunset or sunrise, combining your meditation with yoga practices that help you to feel the balance of the world around you, within you.

TO SUPPORT MOTHER AND FATHER, TO CHERISH PARTNER AND CHILDREN, AND TO BE ENGAGED IN PEACEFUL OCCUPATION - THIS IS THE GREATEST BLESSING

CHAPTER 19

BUDDHISM FOR CHILDREN

"To support mother and father, to cherish partner and children, and to be engaged in peaceful occupation — this is the greatest blessing."

— *The Buddha*

It is amazing that if you step back from your child and really look at how they see the world, which they already encapsulate the Dharma. It is only as they grow and learn from the world around them that they begin to change and the seeds of negative emotion and the search for satisfaction start to grow. What better time to teach the values that the Buddha teaches that when a mind has not yet been thoroughly touched by the world around them? Children are a reflection of what they are taught, the education they receive, and the morals and values of those that they are surrounded by. For anyone that has had the opportunity to travel the world, they quickly see how different cultures and teachings shape young minds into various different ideas.

Incorporating Buddhism into your child's life does not have to start off as intense as teaching them the path to enlightenment, though there is nothing wrong with that if you do. The teachings of the Buddha's of the past and the present allow you to teach your children empathy, understanding, caring for their bodies, and meditation. With meditation alone, you can help your child learn to calm themselves in a world where there is more stimulation from moment to moment than most brains can take in at one time. Naturally, since their children will have questions and you can expound on the story of the first Buddha in a way for a child to understand.

Think of the Christian religion and how in tune the church attempts to be with their youth. The young people are the vessels that will continue the traditions they have set forth. This is the same in Buddhism, however, instead of keeping a religious idea you are making sure that future generations learn the value of morals and empathy, something our world could use today. Even if your child doesn't subscribe to the idea of reincarnation or enlightenment, teaching them to treat all living creatures with care and love will make their lives, and the lives of others, that much purer in this world. Here are some of the basic lessons you can teach your child that is rooted in the Buddhist tradition.

Empathy

In its simplest form, empathy is the ability for someone to share and understand the feelings of others. To empathize with one's joy or one's pain will help keep those negative emotions of anger, jealousy, and revenge from growing with your child as they become adults. Empathy also springs forth the idea of helping others that may be suffering in a way you are not. Allowing your child to think of others before themselves will help them become active participants in the world around them, and in a positive manner. Empathy is the basis of action in Buddhism and should be practiced and taught to everyone that it can be. Teaching does not necessarily mean through words. Many things in life we learn from watching the actions of others, especially our parents. By showing your child that you yourself give empathy to everyone and everything you come in contact with, those actions will be repeated by your child throughout life. Help a child to stand in the footsteps of another to try to come to grips with problems in life and to see those problems through the eyes of compassion.

Environmental Stewardship

If you look at the planet as part of you, you will find that the need to care for it as you would your own body, becomes a priority. Teaching your children the connection they have with the world around them will allow them to see the world as an extension of themselves. Once that is understood then the practice of taking care of the earth, and all the living beings on it will become second nature. Introducing your child to nature in its pure form, from hikes and walks in parks, to trips to other areas less populated than where you are, you will open your child to the understanding that the world is a bigger place than just their backyard. They will begin to feel the natural connection to nature that we all inherently possess. Just as Buddha teaches that you should not mistreat your body, as an extension, you should not abuse the world around you, as we are all connected. Watch as the child learns about rebirth by planting something as simple as an acorn and watching it grow. There is much to be learned from the lifecycle of plants and children love these lessons as much as you love giving them.

Karma

Teaching a child about the concept of Karma can be an enlightening experience in itself if done correctly. You don't want to use Karma as a scare tactic for the child but instead, as a realization that your actions in this life will ultimately affect you at some point. It is important that they know no matter how many good things they do, no matter how much empathy they have, negative things will happen but it how they react to those negative life events that will create a karmic ball rolling in this life and the next. Eventually, your child will do positive things based on their inherent want to them, not out of fear of Karma or negative consequences. Remember that even some of the best deeds done can cause negative consequences somewhere in life. Teaching a child to be loving and giving toward others helps them to appreciate the sentiment of giving without expectations. Giving for giving's sake is part of the Buddhist way of life and they can take pleasure in being compassionate and always ready to give even when the only return is the satisfaction of giving.

Intention

So often we live our lives from moment to moment without really thinking about the things we do or the intention behind them. This is itself can create a plethora of negative consequences and Karma, even if it was not what we set out to do. Remembering your intention in every moment will help you and your child make the choices that best assist in a better world, not just a better life. Remember that once a person has to reach Enlightenment their life does not stop. From there, it is their path to have a positive intention for everything and everyone in the world. Without understanding your own intentions, you will never fully reach that state of bliss. As a child, having positive intention can produce amazing results in everything they do. Let your children feel amazed at the beauty and splendor of the world but let them feel the warm glow inside of themselves that comes from unselfishly helping others in their understanding of life's complexity.

Appreciation

The first Buddha has stated that we need to sit still and relish in every moment in the understanding that we are exactly where we should be. When we get caught up in constantly chasing satisfaction, we forget that the world is moving around us all the time and we are missing it. We want our children's years on this planet to be full of light and happiness and appreciating every moment is an amazing way to feel that fulfillment. An excellent practice you can do with your child is sitting still in your space for meditation. By focusing on the moment around you, controlling your mind from wondering, and just living side by side your child will grow to appreciate each experience they have and allow them to remember their intention. Show the child the wonders of the world. Never be afraid to stop what you are doing to admire the sight of a rainbow or the dance of the raindrops or dewdrops upon the flowers of the garden. A child's natural curiosity and wonderment at life can often be an example to you, as an adult, to appreciate the world in which you live. Children are capable of love and of appreciation that adults often feel biased against or that they resist because of negative experiences within their lives, whereas children are open to love and appreciation of the world that they have in which to grow and to experience life itself.

Meditation

Meditation is not merely reserved for Buddhist but is a fantastic tool for anyone of any faith, religion, or lifestyle. Children can really benefit from, not only the moments of meditation they experience but of the strengthening of the mind, they receive from it. With so much going on in the world, it is essential that each of us understand the place we need to go to in order to balance our bodies and our spirits. Meditation is an excellent technique to teach your child for any situation.

Each day, when they arrive home from school or a trip, take ten to twenty minutes to meditate with your child. Help them understand how to clear their minds, control their anxiety, and reflect on the world around them. By knowing the technique, your child will be able to implement it anywhere at any time, and in a way that no one around them will be able to discern. For example, it's testing day and your child is very nervous, by knowing the technique to calm themselves they will be able to take a moment before the test begins and focus on their breathing, clearing any negative emotion from their bodies. This will help them to really concentrate on the task at hand without the distractions of daily life.

Diversity

In today's world, we have a tendency to see others as different based on their skin color, their background, and their ethnicity. Without even approaching that subject in specifics, and using the education that the Buddha has set forth, you will be able to teach your children to see everyone as the same. By teaching your child the connection they have with everyone and everything, they will begin to see the contents of this planet as an extension of themselves. If you choose to further that by teaching them about reincarnation they will start to understand that the body they possess is just a capsule and that when rebirth takes place, their body could be completely different. This allows them to understand that the outside of someone's person is just a capsule of their inner self. This inner self will come and go in different shapes and personas until they have reached the perfect state of Enlightenment and are released from the cycle of suffering.

Whatever faith, religion, or ideas you have, teaching your children the core principles of Buddhism will help to mold and shape their minds to that closer to their actual self. If they choose to continue the Buddhist way of life you have given them a gift. This gift will make their path to Enlightenment a little easier as their conscious minds are already more in tune with their self. Even if they choose not to follow the Buddhist practice, they will grow into adults that shadow the traits of the true enlightened ones, who travel this earth with empathy and love.

By showing them the way, you cannot force this upon them. You can only hope that they begin to see the light in their own lives and use this for the betterment of their lives and the lives of all who come into contact with them. Meditation isn't easy for a child in the early days although challenged to it in an encouraging way by parents who meditate as well, they are likely to want to do the same things that their parents do and to want to know why these practices are so important to their lives.

CHAPTER 20

YOUR BUDDHIST
HUMAN FORM

"Speak only endearing speech, speech that is welcomed.
Speech, when it brings no evil to others, is a pleasant thing."

— *The Buddha*

As we have explained the body you are in right here and right now is only temporary and when your body dies yourself will be reincarnated into the next. However, that does not give us the go-ahead to treat this body any way we want. The purpose of meditation and everything else is to find true Enlightenment in this lifetime so that you can break the cycle of suffering. Remember that life is the cycle of suffering and we strive to understand fully and reach Nirvana, a state of nothingness and everything at the same time in one lifetime. In order to do that we need to take care of the bodies we have.

Ensuring a longer life will allow you more time to reach your perfect state of enlightenment. A pure and healthy body will also keep all the unneeded chemicals and health issues from clouding your conscious mind and making it difficult to find that place of peace in meditation. Here are some of the different areas of life that will help you understand how to take care of the beautiful human form you have today.

Eating Healthy

It is true that you find that most Buddhists are vegetarians or vegans, but it is not just due to the fact that we are dedicated to bringing no harm to any living creature. Our bodies have been made in a way where, if done correctly, you can live a healthy and happy life on a completely vegetable-based diet. This does not point to a stern belief that you have to live off of raw vegetables, but that you will not include any products that come from an animal and any products that have chemical additives. Despite the public's attempt to push false ideas that eating meat and drinking milk is the only way we can survive, it has been found that eating a vegetable-based diet actually improves your health vastly. This way of eating also reduces your risk of various health conditions such as heart disease and cancer ten-fold.

Our bodies work extra hard to process meats and chemicals. On top of that, the unnatural substances you put in your body also highly affect your mental status as well. For example, I grew up eating meat, drinking three glasses of milk a day, and making a lot of my food from a box. Once I cut all of that out and began making all of my food from scratch and from a vegetable-based diet, my overall health improved, including my ADD and mental issues that included anxiety and depression. Coupling that eating regimen with meditation and my body and mind are so much more at peace.

Exercise

There is nothing wrong with a daily exercise routine, but for this purpose, we are not talking about running out and grabbing the latest workout video. In almost all classes of Buddhism, it is believed to achieve a truly restful mind you have to first get it tired, to begin with. Each day you should be participating in some sort of physical activity from gardening, to hiking, and even walking meditation. This physical exertion will help your restless mind get to a state of peace so that it will be easier for you to meditate.

170

Physical activity is also an amazing way to assist you if you can't seem to calm yourself enough to reach the type of meditative level that you are searching for. Sometimes, when I am unable to focus enough to get into my meditative state fully, I will stop, get up, move around, go for a job, a walk, do some yoga, and other things and then come back to my meditation. If I have had an enormous mental day with work or family, I always have to do something physical in order to prepare my mind for meditation. During these physical activities, I am also allowing my conscious mind to go wherever it would like. In a way, I am allowing the distractions of my ego take over for long enough for it to get out what it is trying to tell me. After that, I am able to calm my conscious state better so that I can better hear my true self.

Vice

Whether it is as dangerous as drugs, alcohol, or smoking, or something smaller scale like sugar and soda, we all struggle with a vice sometime in our lives. These types of stimulants inhibit the mind from becoming clear, ultimately blocking your truth and any chance of Enlightenment. Just like the chemicals that you are intaking in processed meats and foods, these chemical substances, and yes sugar is a chemical, are changing the way your mind works, and creating negative outcomes for your physical body which in turn continues that block. Whatever your vice might be, deciding to quit is one of the best things you can do for your mind, body, and self. A finding has shown that true enlightenment will be absolutely impossible if you are filling your body with negative things.

Think about it this way, every time you put something into your body, a reaction will occur. If you smoke, your lungs will become unhealthy, and addiction will plague your mind. If you put an apple in your body, you will satisfy hunger and provide your body with positive energy. What goes in always comes out in some form or another so take care to curb your vices and give your mind exactly what it needs.

Meditation

If you completely take the search for Enlightenment off the table and focus on the positives of the process of meditation, you will find that it creates a positive outcome for all parts of your sacred body. Your mental and physical status may be thought of as two different things, but they are connected in so many ways. Think about the last time you felt mentally phenomenal, you automatically felt physically amazing as well, and vice versa. Your mind and body go hand and hand with each other. Meditation is a tool that strengthens your control over your mind. When you are able to quiet your mind for meditation you are practicing an ability that can come in handy in everyday life.

I bet that if you think about the last time you got upset about something that later you realized was ridiculous and unneeded. Now imagine that you had such control over your conscious mind that you could realize the error before you allowed to affect the entirety of your body. The situation and your day would have gone a lot differently. Think of your mind, or ego as they call it, as a tool that your body uses. That tool is going to fight for control, but it is not you. When this body dies, and you are reincarnated the only thing you take with you is self or the unconscious truth. Therefore, don't let the ego attached to this body be the hindrance that affects your physical and mental health. Your meditation practice helps you to avoid the pitfalls of everyday existence, such as egoism, selfish endeavor and bigoted opinion which are all contrary to the Buddhist way. When you meditate, you open your mind to whatever may come to it and that enlightenment that makes you into a Buddha in your own right is something that will stay with you for the rest of your life, provided you follow the Buddhist path.

Empathy

Looking at empathy, try to remember what was said above that your mental state affects your physical body and vice versa. Empathy is the ability to feel emotions and to sense what others are feeling as well. This tool can be useful in so many different scenarios. When someone is angry, and you don't know why, but they are taking it out on you, to empathize that they are upset about something is much better than becoming defensive. Ultimately, what you are doing is putting yourself in their shoes for a moment.

Think about how many circumstances you have gone through in your life that would be improved if you were able to step back from your own ego and empathize with the other person. This empathy can lead you into areas of life that you didn't realize or have the patience for before. Looking at both sides of the fence brings about what we are all searching for, to begin with, and that is the truth. Pure truth. With the knowledge of the truth, you can realize what is best not what is "right" in your perspective. What is best is quality in its purest form void of political, social, and personal opinions. Regardless of how you feel about something that doesn't make it the truth. Empathy can help you begin to discern between what you want to see and what is really there.

As with anything else in life, taking care of your body and mind, and breaking yourself from the cycle of negative action can be difficult to do. This is the point in which your practice of intention plays a huge role in helping you through this. If you know what your intentions are, both physically and mentally, you will be able to remind yourself each time you look to partake in something that could be damaging to your Buddhist human form. We understand fully that completely changing your eating habits can be hard, but you will notice as you change and you start eating new and healthy things your body will crave them. It should be a sign to you that when you eat animal products and chemicals you don't get sick when you add in veggies, but when you eat a vegetable-based diet, and you randomly add in one of the above, your body rejects it. The same goes for vice and negative thought. As you go along, it will become 100% natural to practice these actions.

Humility

I have added the quality of humility for a very specific purpose. Humility is your ability to accept that you are one small, ever-changing part of the universe in which you live your life. This humility enables you rather than holds you back. When you approach life in a mindful way, it doesn't matter how important the task. It has the same significance and you do it with a humble heart, not expecting returns or rewards, but merely because the task has to be done.

One of the most humbling experiences of my life was actually cleaning up the floor of an ashram in Tibet where I was a guest. I was having problems with silencing the mind until that moment. Over the course of a week, I had been struggling with the difficult task of being mindful because I was trying too hard. Often, when you are faced with a challenge in life, you believe that you need to put conscious effort into that challenge to make it work correctly. I explain this for a specific purpose. When you try to meditate, sometimes you are so busy pushing yourself that you are unable to draw from the humility of the experience. On this particular day, I was asked to clean a floor. The jobs were done in silence and normally, as the floor was cleaned, thought processes came and went but on this particular day, I had been told by my guru that it wasn't trying that got you into a state of meditation. It was being able to let go and to let the mind do what it needed to do. Thus, as I cleaned, I allowed the experience to absorb me. I could see the cloth on the floor of the ashram and could see how the water made the tiles glisten in the sunlight. I could see the dirt of footmarks and I could see them slowly being moved away by the cloth that I was using.

When you approach meditation in a humble way and are able to put aside all of the problems of life which seem to be overbearingly important and you become humbled by the experience of meditation, you are able to let go of your concepts and start to embrace the mindful approach that helps you to reach that moment of awakening. If you really want to know what true meditation feels like and are having difficulty with it, then a humble approach to a relatively simple but necessary task can help you to let go of your suppositions and be suspended in that moment in the most mindful of ways. Apart from achieving a very clean floor, I also achieved a very receptive heart and that's what the guru was trying to help me to achieve. It was dropping my own importance and taking the stance of humility that allowed me to see the light, and it can do the same thing for you.

Meditate...
do not delay,
lest you later regret it.

- The Buddha

CHAPTER 21

DIFFERENT BUDDHIST RITUALS

Meditate... do not delay, lest you later regret it.

– The Buddha

Buddhism, having been around for so long, is saturated in traditions and rituals. A ritual can be as simple as meditation or as elaborate as the ceremonial blessing of the Buddha statue. You don't have to participate in these rituals just because you are following a Buddhist lifestyle but if you wish to immerse yourself in the traditions fully, they are pertinent parts of the Buddhist way of life. Though some of these rituals will be explained below, it is not nearly the extent of how Buddhists pay homage to the Buddha and to their heritage. If you are interested in learning the more sacred rituals, it is advised to contact your local temple and seek the guidance of a teacher.

As you take in the information in this chapter, you will hear words such as blessings and reverence but remember they are not connected to worship. Instead, most of the traditions of Buddhism are there to show thanks to the Buddha for his teachings and his guidance. Just as you would thank a teacher in school, the Buddhists find that paying homage to Buddha for his lessons is pertinent since they will lead to the end of their suffering in the cycle of life. You may choose to participate in these or just silently and personally give thanks for the Buddha's teachings. Here are some of the rituals practiced in Buddhism.

Bowing

Bowing is a simple tradition, also known as prostration, and is done each time that you approach a likeness of the Buddha in a place of meditation or teaching. Each person is supposed to prostrate three times by kneeling on a stool in front of the Buddha with both of your palms facing up. During the first bow, turning of one hand represents the cultivation of wisdom inside you, while the other represents the offering of compassion to others. Therefore, your open palms mean wisdom and compassion. You may also bow when you are done with yoga or meditation sessions if it seems correct in that situation. Giving thanks to the Buddha will not be frowned upon. It may even light that spark of hope within your heart that your meditation will be fruitful and that you will learn the ways of Buddha with the respect that these lessons should be approached with.

Chants

You may be familiar with rhythmic sounds of monks chanting in the temples. Chanting is more than just singing it is the representation and reminder to live a life discipline, perseverance, and charity. These things are brought to light through chanting which is the repetitious singing of Buddha's teachings. The sound itself can be found to be soothing and close to the universal sound of connectivity to the earth, or Ohm, as the Buddhist practice refers to it. However, there is no particular pitch or tone that is required for chanting, and these chants can be done at any time during a ceremony or before and after meditation. Oftentimes when meditating with a teacher, they will chant during your meditation as a way to remember the Buddha's teachings and bring the true self closer to the realization of Enlightenment.

Gongs and Singing Bowls

These instruments are used for several different things. In ceremony gongs and singing bowls are used to signal the beginning or end of a teaching or event. During meditation, they are used to begin meditation by creating a universal tone to focus. They are also used to end the meditation and bring the practitioner carefully from their rested state. Gongs are also specifically used during chanting to aid in focus, tone, and remembrance. Many people choose to have these types of instruments in their personal meditation space, though usually on a much smaller scale than what can be found in a temple. However, they are useful to remind practitioners of the seriousness of the process of meditation and to start the session with a traditional opening and then close the session in a similar way.

The Lighting of Incense

Incense is not just used as a fragrant appliance during meditation; it is also used in ritual. The lighting of the incense is a reminder for you to break free from the cycle of life, suffering, death, and rebirth. It is an homage you pay to the original true teacher as he guides you on your path to freedom through his teachings. They lit incense also plays as a focal point during meditation to help guide you into a deeper state of stillness.

Buddhists also use lit incense as an offering to the Buddha in exchange for his blessing on their path. Though Buddha is not seen as a being like the Christian God, some do worship him as their leader in the path to Enlightenment. How you personally choose to use the tool is entirely personal and up to you and your beliefs.

Offerings on the Altar

If you visit a temple, you will often find offerings laid on a table for the Buddha in thanks. These offerings are usually fruit, flowers, or sometimes vegetarian dishes. The Chinese New Year is a time of great offerings as thanks to the Buddha for his guidance through the last year. You can create offerings of your own in your home meditation space. When the offerings begin to wilt or decay you can simply remove them and discard them in the manner in which you feel most comfortable. Offerings also don't have to be what is listed above as some use branches, rocks, and other natural finds as offerings in a showing of connectivity with the world around you. If you care to create your own meditation area in your garden, choose a Buddha with a bowl and as the different flowers come out in the garden, you can offer fresh flowers to the Buddha before you start your meditation and thus mix your enjoyment of nature with your enjoyment of sharing and learning to take your meditational practice seriously. When a flower wilts, then replace it with a fresh one and keep your altar alive, encouraging yourself to be reminded of your Buddhist ways.

Taking Refuge

The Buddhist tradition of taking refuge does not mean that you shut yourself away, but instead that you immerse yourself completely in Buddhism. You take a vow of sorts to live the complete life of a Buddhist no matter what life may throw at you. The ceremony is for those that are deeply spiritual and connected to Buddhism and is performed by your teacher. It is necessary, at this level, to have a teacher who can show you and teach you everything that is involved in giving yourself to Buddhism. This is not something to take lightly or do on a whim; it is a commitment. It said that when one takes refuge, the teachings and learned an understanding of the Buddhist path will travel with you to the next life. You are not required to change your friends, your faith, or anything of that nature, but you are vowing to live a life for the positive forward progression of others.

The ceremony of taking refuge can be a bit long but thoroughly explains your duties as a Buddhist and offers the protection of Buddha himself. At the end of the ceremony, the different teachers or monks will drape a white or blue scarf over your shoulders as a sign of respect and protection. You will also receive a traditional Buddhist name different from your own, and it is assigned during this ritual.

Confession

Confession may be a familiar word to those who are familiar with the Christian religion or Catholics. However, it does not hold the same connotation in Buddhism. Confession is simply a way, through prayer, or speaking to a teacher or monk, to allow yourself to be released from guilt so that you may be able to see the truth behind the actions. Buddha cannot dissolve your transgression, but he does not scorn either. Karma is set in stone, a consequential chain of events that even the Buddha cannot disrupt. Therefore, confession itself is used as a tool to teach you of the ego behind your actions, the outcome of negativity, and how to approach the same situation in the Buddhist way. You don't always have to talk to someone, which is where prayer comes into play. You release your guilt, suffering, to the Buddha, and in return begin to understand the truth behind your actions.

It is important to remember Karma and how for every good deed you will find light and happiness, and for every bad one, Karma will reap its revenge. That in itself sounds terrifying, but we must remember that there is equal reaction to every action. As we talked about with vice in the previous chapter, there is a reaction to every action, sometimes good and sometimes bad depending on the action. This is the same for Karma. Confession does not clear you of this, but that is not what it is about, it is about learning and growing in self so that you will eventually reach that state of Enlightenment. You may find that confession in your own space at home will assist you to make your life's journey more in keeping with the Nobel Eight Fold Path and can study your own progress as you go through your meditation by keeping a journal of the confessions that are hindering your process. If you do not wish to write them down, at least, saying them can help you to reap the benefits of understanding and learning what you are doing in your life that may be blocking your route toward enlightenment.

Precept Ceremony

The Precept Ceremony is almost always included in and associated with Taking Refuge. However, it is also often done at the end of other ceremonies. The person involved is relaying and taking oath in the five precepts which connect with the Three Truths. This ceremony is the most commonly performed ritual in Buddhism and shows the devotion of the attendee to the Buddhist practice. The monk or teacher performing the ritual often covers their face with a fan that demonstrates the ceremony as general instead of personal. The relationship between the teacher and student has nothing to do with the act of relaying the precepts and should be done by any person giving their vow and devotion to Buddhist ways. This ceremony, unlike others, must be done by a higher member of a Buddhist community or temple.

Dedication of Merit

The Dedication of Merit is one of the very actions of Buddhism that shows the care and love of the world and living beings around us. It is the process of sharing all the good, all the teachings, and all the merit that one has collected with the world. The process involves thinking, or wishing, one singular, extraordinary outcome for the world and pushing that out in the universe using your collected positives as weight. This process is completely selfless and should be entered into with no self-serving thoughts at all. Not only does this create a positive effect in the universe but it also teaches the person how to give with no selfish undertones. The Dedication of Merit can be done as a ceremony or simply through stillness and meditation internally.

It is important to understand, however, that this dedication, if done with malice, negativity, or selfishness will not only fail to work, but will also create a Karmic backlash in your direction. Giving during dedications, prayer, and everyday acts should be done as you want to create positivity in the world, not in your own life. Karma recognizes self-serving acts; you cannot fool the universe. This is part of the Enlighted path and shows how once you reach that heightened level, each and everything you do will come naturally as a selfless act.

Meditation

The last ritual we will talk about has been spoken about throughout this book but has not been realized as an actual ritualistic act. Meditation is there to help you learn how to control your conscious mind, explore your true self, and connect the self with the body and the breath. Breathing is an exercise in meditation that cannot be left out. Now, this does not mean that you can, possibly meditate without breathing, this simply means without the focus on breath your meditation will not be full.

You may have a challenging time understanding meditation as a ritual, but if you think about the base of a ritual, it is anything that is repeatedly done in reverence to something or someone else. Meditation is used as a tool to your path to enlightenment and should be done on a daily basis. Meditation is a sacred ritual in the Buddhist way of life and is done several times a day every day in temples and centers. The art of meditation is the key to your Enlightenment, and if nothing else is observed from this chapter, you want to take full advantage of understanding meditation and how to use it in all facets of your life.

Rituals and traditions are longstanding inside of the Buddhist community. Many of these include prayer, devotion, and experience but if they are something that interests you, starting out with a Buddhist lifestyle is the first step. Monks and teachers have devoted their lives to the furthering of the path of Enlightenment and the positive and peaceful spread of knowledge across the globe. Many of these rituals are performed daily, especially meditation, and to watch them occur can be truly life-changing. After you set up your home meditation space and begin to study further into a life in the Buddhist practice, you will find that some of these you do without even thinking about it. Each day bowing has become part of my routine and not out of habit but out of thankfulness for the teachings that the first Buddha laid out for the world.

The truth is something that is hidden in all of the Enlightenment and us is something that can be achieved through dedication and an open self. The calm and real life of a Buddhist is one that lacks selfishness, adverse actions, and disrespect. Through empathy, love, and peace the Buddha will guide you through the steps and lessons that you will need to take with you each and every day from the time you wake in the morning until you rest your head at night. These lessons will infiltrate past your conscious mind and go right to the heart of your true self, allowing for an opening in your life that will only be filled with real and unrepented kindness towards others. Remember, we are all creatures of the same earth, connected through a string that leads us from birth to death and back again.

CONCLUSION

I hope that after reaching this section, many of your questions about Buddhism have been answered. You may have discerned as well that the primary purpose of the First Buddha to have taught his discoveries was to help others.

Now, the best way to put all of his teachings to good use is to practice them in everyday life. After all, the Buddha himself explained that the only way to understand Buddhism is to walk the path yourself.

However, it is completely normal to stray from the path that the Buddha had so carefully advised one to follow. This is especially true in the modern world, which is filled with distractions and desires. Therefore, to help you stay motivated to practice what you have just learned each day, here are some pieces of advice:

First, begin each day with a prayer of intention. Have a morning mantra that you can softly declare to yourself each morning to cultivate thoughts of loving-kindness.

Second, set an appointment with yourself each day, for meditation. Making time to nourish your spirit and mind through mindfulness meditation is not unlike finding the time to eat your meals. Perhaps a good time to start meditation is in the morning, shortly after waking up. Try it and notice how it makes you feel each day.

The third is to remind yourself of the basic principles of Buddhism throughout your day. It can be challenging at times, especially when your mind is filled with your responsibilities. However, it starts with simply telling yourself, "I do not want to harm anyone with my thoughts, words, and actions." By doing so, you become more mindful of your choices and would be more likely to choose what is good.

Last is to spend a few minutes at the end of each day to practice mindfulness. It is usually during this time when people feel the least motivated and willful because of exhaustion. However, it also presents the perfect opportunity to reflect on how the day was for you and what you can learn from these experiences. You could even discover more about yourself by doing so.

Aside from these, there are plenty of other ways for you to incorporate the teachings of the Buddha in your life.

Just take it one step at a time.

Finally, if you enjoyed this book, then I'd like to ask you for a favor, would you be kind enough to leave a review for this book on Amazon? It would be **greatly appreciated!**

Simply go to **bit.ly/BuddhismReview** to leave a review for this book on Amazon.

I would love for you to connect with me on Social Media with any comments, questions or just to experience beautiful images and quotes.

My Instagram: @Yogitation
My publishing account on Instagram: @QualityChapters
My publishing account on Facebook: Quality Chapters

If you're looking for books that inspire you and helps you enjoy life more, head on over to www.QualityChapters.com

Thank you and good luck,
Michael Williams

Don't forget to get your FREE Bonus Gift!

Thanks again for taking your time to download and read my book, and I want you to continue on your path to a more peaceful and enjoyable life, so I want to give you the **"Yoga For All: The Simple Guide To Yoga & Meditation"** e-book for FREE!

Go to **bit.ly/freebookyoga** to download the FREE e-book.

Also, sign up for my Email list to get updates, new releases, and notifications when my books are on sale as well as FREE!

Preview of

BUDDHISM FOR BEGINNERS

How to Go from Beginner to Monk and Master Your Mind

INTRODUCTION

The common idea which most people possess is that Buddhism is an ancient religion, belonging to antique temples, mystics, history woven with fiction, and the ways of the old. True enough, Buddhism is a religion and it's around 2,500 years old. But more importantly, Buddhism is a way of life. And from where you are at the moment, Buddhism is a spiritual journey. The goal of this book is to light your path. Through this book, you will learn what Buddhism is truly about, who Buddha really was, and what his teachings were. This book also hopes to shed light on the common misconceptions surrounding Buddhism.

That said, the most distinctive feature of this book is that it will help you see how the teachings from thousands of years ago apply to the world we live in today. These pages contain everything that a beginner in Buddhism should know, from the basic beliefs of Buddhism to the concepts of Reincarnation and Karma to the Roots of Evil. You'll find that the explanations of the principles and beliefs are presented in simple, easy-to-understand terms. That's because, in Buddhism, practice is just as important as philosophy. Get a vivid glimpse of a day in the life of a Buddhist. More importantly, learn how you can apply the teachings of Buddha in your daily life.

Throughout your journey to enlightenment, treat this book as your faithful companion, the torch to give light when the path is shadowy when the wisdom of the Buddha is hard to understand and even more difficult to follow.

Meditation plays a vital role in Buddhism. Your thoughts possess unlimited power to shape the world. Learn how to master your mind, to understand the universe, and to use your thoughts to ease suffering and to achieve ultimate peace and happiness.

CHAPTER 1

THE WORLD OF
BUDDHISM

Buddhism Demystified: What Is Buddhism?

Buddhism is a religion, a philosophy, and a lifestyle. The name comes from the word "budhi" which translates to "to awaken." It was 2,500 years ago when the Buddha, known then as Siddhartha Gautama, experienced the awakening himself and thus founded Buddhism. As mentioned in the introduction, Buddhism is more than just a religion. In order to be a practicing Buddhist, you must:

- Lead a moral existence

- Develop awareness and practice mindfulness in your everyday thoughts and deeds

- Practice the virtues of wisdom and understanding

To become a Buddhist is to understand the world, to appreciate its beauty, and to comprehend its injustices. To become a Buddhist is to develop respect for the world and for all that dwells in it, and to recognize the interconnection between all living beings. Buddhism will help you see the purpose of life. When you follow Buddhism's code of practice, it will inevitably lead you to a genuinely happy, meaningful, and fulfilled existence.

The reason why Buddhism has continued to thrive throughout the centuries is that the ancient teachings of the Buddha continue to provide generation after generation with simple answers which address the very root of their problems. Whether the problem is physical illness, emotional emptiness, spiritual starvation, psychological issues, or social conflict, Buddhism holds the solution for them all.

As history shows, clinging to religion has helped various groups of people to cope with the difficulties they experienced in this world. Buddhism has done the same and has never stopped to do so. Its philosophies have never ceased to remain relevant. That's because Buddhism recognizes that the root of human suffering throughout history is always the same. Therefore, the solution, too, is constant. In other words, the teachings of the Buddha remain applicable even to contemporary societies. In a modern world plagued with materialism, there is a greater need to learn and to live out the philosophies of Buddhism.

What makes Buddhism different from other religions?

Unlike most major religions, Buddhism does not focus on worshipping an omnipresent, omniscient, and omnipotent supernatural being. Even though some Buddhists revere gods and celestial Buddhas, the religion itself is not centered on one "Supreme Being" which is the embodiment of "all that is good." Furthermore, it does not recognize the existence of a superlative evil which is the personification of "all that is bad." And more importantly, Buddhism is not predominantly a system of belief. Though Buddhists are taught certain doctrines, students of Buddhism are urged to avoid following in blind faith.

Buddhism recognizes that human beings possess the capacity to distinguish between good and evil. Simply put, Buddhism promotes the use of human intelligence as well as your freedom to choose. You are encouraged to possess an open mind and an open heart. However, you are also encouraged to employ skepticism when it is necessary. The Dalai Lama of Tibet couldn't have said it better: If the teachings suit you, then incorporate them into your life using the best of your capabilities. If, however, the teachings don't suit you, then just leave them be.

The Buddha himself told his followers not to embrace everything he says merely because he said it. He advised them to test his teachings as though examining the authenticity of gold. If, after a thorough examination, his teachings proved to be true, then the followers may put them to practice.

You can see now the appeal of Buddhism as a religion. It doesn't command. It doesn't demand. Buddhism doesn't provide you with the illusion that you were born free and then enslave you with rules that are set in stone. It does not tell you that you are a creature of intelligence and then confuse you by setting limits on what you can do. More importantly, it does not tell you that you are loved and yet frighten you with ideas of eternal damnation.

Instead, Buddhism encourages you to become the best version of yourself, to utilize your inborn capacities as a human being, and to maximize these potentials to create a better world than the one you have found.

Like other religions, Buddhism strives to help you find the answers to the deeper questions in life such as "Who am I?" and "How can I be happy?" But the wonderful thing about Buddhism is that it doesn't just ask you to do this and that, take the Buddha's word for it and then leave you to try to make sense of it all. Instead, Buddhism invites you to *personally experience* the nature of reality for yourself.

Once you are *awakened* or *enlightened*, you will be able to experience your internal reality as well as your external reality. That internal reality is that part of you which remains constant and untouched by the external world. Think of it as your anchor which will keep you steady despite the chaos of the world around you. Think of it as the lotus which will remain untainted even as you float along a polluted pond.

The ultimate goal of Buddhism is to enable you to experience *the awakening* in the very same way as the Buddha had.

If Buddhists don't worship a Supreme Being, who was Buddha, then?

To get straight to the point, Buddha was a man who lived in the 5th century BCE. He was born as a man, he lived as a man, and then like all mortal men, he passed away. Nevertheless, he was immortalized in the memory of his disciples because of the extraordinary life that he had lived.

He was born into the royal family of the Shakya clan in what is known today as Nepal. Despite the fact that he was able to experience all the sensual delights that the world had to offer, Prince Siddhartha, as he was then called, had deep compassion for his suffering brethren. Even when surrounded with luxuries, he understood the universality of sorrow. At age 29, he abandoned his wealth and all worldly pleasures. At the prime of his life, he chose to lead an austere existence. He wore a simple yellow garment and, without a penny to his name, roamed the world in a quest for Peace, Truth, and Freedom from Suffering.

For six years straight, he prayed and performed self-mortification. He tormented his body in an attempt to nourish the soul. He did this until he reached the point of emaciation. It was then that he realized that the severities which he practiced were useless. Through his personal experience, he was able to ascertain that self-mortification only served to weaken the body and consequently, exhaust the spirit. He then used this experience to form an independent path. This is when he found the Majjhima Patipada, also known as the Middle Path.

Enlightenment came to him as he was meditating under the Bodhi tree. It was at this moment that he awakened to Buddhahood. From then on, he became known as Shakyamuni Buddha or "the awakened wise man of the Shakya Clan." He did this all on his own, as a man with no supernatural powers.

For the next 45 years of his existence, the Buddha dedicated his life to preaching all over the North Indian subcontinent. He taught whoever that was interested in living a life free from suffering.

He was 80 years old when he died. The Buddha was mortal and yet he was godlike in every respect. However, despite the fact that he had plenty of followers who revered him, he was never so arrogant as to refer to himself as a divine being.

The bottom line is that the Buddha was human, much like you and me. And like him, we, too, can achieve awakening. *Like him, we, too, can become Buddhas.* As a Bodhisatta (an aspiring Buddha), you, too, can follow that path which the Buddha has led and in so doing, find Truth, Peace, and Freedom from Suffering. The Buddha pointed out that we shall find salvation only by relying on ourselves, on our own capabilities, and on our own efforts. Simply put, *you are your own savior.*

Common Misconceptions about Buddhism

- **Buddhism is not about living in extremes.**

When you look at the portrayal of the Buddha in art galleries or in pop culture, you'll see a stark, cold, lifeless effigy with an emotionless, though serene countenance. It sucks the fun out of wanting to be a Buddha, doesn't it?

But as Siddhartha Gautama found out 2,500 years ago, self-deprivation is not the path towards enlightenment. Take a look at the face of the 14th Dalai Lama. He's always smiling, brimming with energy, and radiating with the beauty of life. *This* is the true face of Buddhism. Buddhists are encouraged to laugh, to love, to enjoy life. The whole purpose of the awakening is not just to end suffering but also to achieve indescribable joy.

The joy to be found in monastic Buddhism is not in the strictness of routine, but in the awareness, the wisdom, and the purity that a simple life brings. Devoid of the distractions of postmodern existence, spiritual awareness arrives more quickly and more clearly.

What about those monks who burned themselves to death?

Self-immolation is known as putting an end to one's life as a form of sacrifice. Perhaps you have seen circulating videos of Buddhist monks burning themselves to death while retaining meditative postures. To some, this shows self-transcendence. But in truth, not all Buddhists agree with this kind of sacrifice.

Contrary to what the media might have you believe, Buddhists do not possess this morbid fixation on suffering and death. Suicide is generally not recommended in Buddhism. It may be performed but only if a good reason exists (e.g. if you truly believe that your death will save someone else's life). Whether the reason is good enough or not, it all depends entirely on you.

Vietnamese monk and teacher Thich Nhat Hanh were reported to have said to Martin Luther King, Jr. that burning oneself is a way of proving that what one is saying is of the highest importance. Again, not all Buddhists agree with this. As mentioned earlier, if the teaching suits you, follow it. If it doesn't, leave it alone.

The bottom line is that those monks burned themselves not because they wished to embrace death more than life. They did so because, in their hearts, they believed that their sacrifice would create a positive difference in the world.

- **Buddhism is not strictly for Asians.**

Buddhism is not exclusive to a single race, country, or group of people. Over the centuries, a great portion of the Western population has benefitted from the teachings of the Buddha.

Celebrities practicing Buddhism include Angelina Jolie, Brad Pitt, Orlando Bloom, Sting, Naomi Watts, Keanu Reeves, Tiger Woods, Richard Gere, and more.

Suffering is universal. People all over the globe suffer from pain, sorrow, emptiness, destructive behavior, and unhealthy thoughts and emotions. The wisdom of the Buddha and the experience of the awakening are open to everyone and anyone who wishes to benefit from it. Likewise, the teachings of Buddhism are applicable to the life of any person who desires to achieve lifelong happiness, mindfulness, wisdom, compassion, and peace of mind.

- **Buddhism is not about idol worship.**

When you enter a Buddhist temple, you'll see numerous statues, incense being burned, flowers being offered, and monks prostrating themselves in front of the altar. Even so, Buddhists do not worship Buddhas in the same way as followers of other faiths worship their gods. Prostration in Buddhism is performed as a conscientious deed as opposed to being a mindless ritualistic act.

Bowing

Buddhist monks tend to bow a great deal. As a Westerner, who was raised to "bow down to no one," this practice may be difficult to embrace. However, bowing serves as a way of conveying that you willingly give up your self-centered preoccupation.

There are times when Buddhist monks are required to bow (e.g. when facing the altar). However, Buddhists monks don't always bow because they *have* to. Often, they do this because they *want* to. It is the best way to express their gratitude, their respect, and their acknowledgement to their teachers, to the Buddhas, and even to their robes. When monks and nuns and laypersons bow to each other as a sign of respect, this helps create an atmosphere of love and harmony. So open your mind and rid yourself of Western prejudices. Understand that when you bow to show your respect to others, you are, in a way, respecting yourself.

Furthermore, the act of bowing in Buddhism reveals the strong influence of Asian culture in the religion. For instance, in Southeast Asia, one way of showing your respect is to hold your hands together as though in prayer and then raise them to your slightly lowered forehead. A full bow is done by assuming a kneeling position while sitting on your buttocks. Next, you place your palms flat on the floor, 4 inches apart from each other. Then, you bend to touch your forehead to the floor.

A half bow is usually performed in Japanese Zen. This is done by keeping your hands together, as though in prayer, and placing them in front of your chest. Then, you bend your body from the waist. A full bow is performed by assuming a kneeling position while sitting on your buttocks. Then, you hold your palms skyward.

- **Buddhists don't think that everything is an illusion.**

What the teachers actually mean to say is: Everything is *like* an illusion.

One of the goals of Buddhism is to teach people to see past the world of appearances and to let go of insubstantial dreams. Such worldly illusions are one of the primary causes of human suffering.

People tend to erroneously interpret this teaching as "nothing in this world really exists." This kind of thinking is potentially dangerous and can steer an aspiring Buddhist such as you towards the wrong path.

If nothing in this world is real, then nothing matters. But the world *is* real. And we do live in a universe that is ruled by the law of cause and effect. However, everything is *not always as they seem*. The physical world as you see it may be made up of separate entities. You look down at your body and see an autonomous being. You look at your pet and see a separate being. You look at a rock and see a solid object. And each of you appears to be detached from each other.

However, in reality, everything is connected with each other through an intricate web. Thus, every word that you say, every deed you perform, and every thought that forms in your mind will inevitably affect the world. As an aspiring Buddhist, you are urged to recognize this interconnectedness so that it may guide you in your way of life.

- **Being a Buddhist doesn't mean that you can't get angry**

Often, Buddhists use meditation as a means to overcome negative emotions such as anger. For this reasons, Buddhists are often pictured as placid individuals who are able to remain calm and collected even during the worst of times. However, becoming a Buddhist monk doesn't mean that you can instantaneously get rid of negative thoughts or habits. Let's get real. Monks are human beings, too. And so was the Buddha, for that matter. That said, as an aspiring Buddhist, one of your goals is to allow your actions to be guided by the power of love. This means showing kindness even to your enemies. This means seeing the wisdom behind every adversity.

This, however, doesn't mean that you should allow other people to walk all over you. To be Buddhist is not about *ignoring* the wrong deed but to *actively* do what you can to change or stop the other person's bad behavior. You do this in a non-violent way and as guided by the spirit of compassion. Simply put, whatever action you take, it should be constructive rather than destructive.

CHAPTER 2

A JOURNEY TOWARDS ENLIGHTENMENT

What are the basics beliefs of Buddhism?

While resting under the shade of a tree, the Buddha marveled at the beauty of the countryside. Yet, underneath all this beauty, he saw unhappiness. He recognized it in the way the farmer beat his ox, in the way the trees shed their leaves so that new ones may grow, and in the way a bird fed on a worm, and so on. To himself, he asked: "Why must one creature suffer so that the other may prosper? Why must one living being die in order for another to survive?" During the period of his awakening, the Buddha found the answers to these questions.

The Three Universal Truths

- **Nothing in this universe is ever lost.**

Matter transforms into energy. Likewise, energy transforms into matter. Corporeal bodies turn to dust. Solar systems crumble and become cosmic rays. The old dies so that it may give way to the new.

Each living being is interconnected. Each living being is equal. But more than that, each living being is *the same*. To destroy something from nature is to destroy oneself. To harm another is to harm oneself. It is for this reason that Buddhists neither hurt nor kill animals.

- **Everything is subject to change.**

The world and everything in it are constantly changing. Life is a river that goes on and on. Sometimes, it flows slowly. Sometimes, it flows with a fury. In some places, it flows smoothly. But there are areas too

195

that are stony.

What was regarded as reality hundreds of years ago may be false today. What was true yesterday may not be true today? Once, we were convinced that the world was flat. Once, no one ever dreamed of the possibility of flight. Life and our ideas about it change ever so constantly.

- **Everything is influenced by cause and effect.**

The reason for the constant change mentioned above is the law of cause and effect. During his awakening under the Bodhi tree, the Buddha's previous lives unraveled before his eyes and so he was able to see the pattern of cause and effect.

In this universe, one gets what he deserves. One reaps the fruit of the seed which he had sown. Who you are now is the product of your thoughts. Through your thoughts, emotions, and actions, you have the power to achieve the kind of life that you desire. Therefore, if you want good things to come to you, you must bear positive thoughts and emotions. If you wish to receive kindness, then you yourself must show kindness.

Karma and Why You've Been Looking At It The Wrong Way

Contrary to what most people might think, the Law of Karma is not something to fear. It is not a theory made up to frighten people into obedience. It is but a simple fact of the universe. It exists and operates just as the law of gravity does. As a Buddhist, you are urged not to regard karma as a form of punishment for evil deeds. Instead, you are to look upon it as an opportunity to build a brighter future, rather like a simple formula for a blissful existence.

The word karma literally translates into "action." But most people tend to mistakenly regard it as "fate." You might've heard someone say: "My life sucks because this is my karma." When you look at it this way, you make karma seem unpredictable, vague, and unchangeable.

On the contrary, karma is dynamic, foreseeable, and clear as crystal. You are aware that every day, each action you make, be it positive or negative, will inevitably find its way back to you. If you plant a cabbage, you don't expect a carrot to grow back, do you? Even now, you *know* what's going to happen in the future. You *know* what seed you've sown and as such, you know what fruit you shall be reaping. But more importantly, you have the power to control your karma. Your karma is constantly changing. Each waking moment, each opportunity to act provides you with a fresh chance to turn karmic results in your favor. So if you think that your job is to sit there and passively accept what the universe gives you, think again. We were all born to be the masters of our destinies. It is up to you to create the kind of life that you want.

As mentioned, karma is not a system of punishment or reward (e.g. If you tell a lie, you'll be born a cripple in your next life. If you help a neighbor in need, you'll be rewarded with riches). The universe isn't judgmental or shallow like that.

Also, more important than your actions are your *intentions*. So if you accidentally step on a bug, relax. You won't be born as an insect in your next life. However, if you squash the bug on purpose, especially out of anger or malevolence, expect appropriate karmic consequences to be executed.

The rule is simple: Act with hate, and you'll attract negative things. Act with love, and you'll attract positive things.

What if you do something truly terrible, like kill someone?

When you brutally murder someone, expect to experience the consequences in this life or in the next. In this life, you may know immense sorrow. Or in your next life, you may be birthed into a world of extreme suffering. If you do nothing to cleanse your karma through positive acts, the heavier the consequences grow.

Furthermore, your state of mind when performing the terrible act makes all the difference in the immensity of the karma that you collect. For instance, if you kill out of self-defense, the karmic consequences may be lighter. But if you kill out of envy, anger, or for the sheer delight of it, then the consequences are naturally heavier.

So if I see people suffering in this lifetime, does that mean they did something in their past lives to deserve it?

When someone is suffering in this lifetime, treat him as you are supposed to: with compassion. Find a glimmer of happiness and hope in knowing that even as they are suffering, at least they are being given the chance to cleanse their karma. This way, they will be able to enjoy a better life when they are reborn.

Born Again and Again: Understanding Rebirth

Death is but an impermanent end to an impermanent existence.

Through powerful meditation, one has the capability to recall one's past lives. If you possess this ability, you'll be able to put your present life into a meaningful perspective.

Karma and Reincarnation provide us with a plausible explanation for inequality. It shows why some men are born rich while others are born poor, why some babies are healthy while others are handicapped. For some, this may be a pretty hard pill to swallow.

The condition to which you have been born reflects the lesson that you need to learn in this lifetime. For instance, a person may be born rich because it is most important for him to learn the value of generosity. Alternatively, a person may be born poor because it is most important for him to learn the value of hard work.

A common question asked by skeptics is this: If our souls never truly die and if we are constantly reborn in each lifetime, then how does that explain the fact that the world is more populated today than it was decades ago?

The human realm is but one of many other realms. When we pass on, we may end up in other realms. There are heavenly realms and lower realms. There are animal realms and ghostly realms. Likewise, beings from other realms may also be reborn into the human realm. Simply put, you could've been dwelling in another realm before you were reborn here in your present life. By understanding that we continuously come and go between these various realms, we gain deeper respect and empathy for other beings.

The Three Marks of Existence

Buddhists believe that everything that exists in this world is subject to the following:

- **Anicca**

Impermanence

Everything in this universe has its limitation. Everything exists in its own duration. When something appears, it will inevitably disappear just as surely as it had materialized.

You look around you and you see solid objects. You derive comfort and safety from their solidity, from their permanence. However, as previously mentioned, nothing is ever as it seems. Deep inside, you *know* that nothing in this world is permanent and yet often, you choose to ignore that knowledge. That is where the problem lies. In order to successfully detach yourself from the material world, it is necessary to acknowledge anicca. However, if you continue to nurture this kind of primordial ignorance, you will continue to fall prey to the poisons of hatred and envy.

• Dukkha

Suffering

Nothing is ever meant to be satisfactory. Thus, you must learn to depend on nothing, whether it's a physical object, a person, or an emotion. A happy moment, no matter how beautiful, will not last. Success will eventually fade. This mark of existence, like the previous one, is closely related to the ephemeral nature of things. The Buddha teaches you to cling to nothing.

That said, it does not mean that you are not allowed to enjoy success, happiness, or prosperity. In fact, you are encouraged to relish each wonderful moment in your life. Enjoy it *but* never cling to it. Later, we will discuss Mindfulness and how it can help you live a happier, fuller life.

• Anatta

There is no "I"

There is no such thing as "the self." You are not an individual entity. Hence, you should also refrain from viewing other beings and things as separate entities. And since they are not separate entities, they can neither be owned nor controlled. Since "the self" is not real but merely an illusion, you cannot own yourself. Thus, you cannot control yourself.

Nothing in this world is permanent. That includes your "self" as you perceive it. And that which is not permanent only serves to cause you pain. Why? Because you tend to hold onto it. And when you feel that it's gone, that is, when you can no longer perceive it through your physical senses, then you experience a sense of loss, a feeling of grief.

Would you willingly place your hand on a pile of burning coal knowing that it will hurt you? Of course not! So why attempt to hold something knowing that it will only serve to hurt you in the long run? To attempt to hold, own, or control anything will inevitably lead to suffering. This is because you hold on to an illusion but the moment you lose it, you experience pain as though the object of your mourning really did exist.

Do you see now how people subject themselves needlessly every day to suffering? And it's all because they cling to delusions.

But wait, didn't you just say that we are the masters of our destinies? How can we make our own fate when we cannot own and control ourselves?

What the Buddha wishes you to understand is that the absolute absence of control is the only path towards mastery. When you acknowledge the impermanence of things when you embrace the fact that the "I" does not exist, and when you learn to depend on nothing, then it is *you who controls your life* as opposed to the *illusions controlling you.*

The Four Noble Truths

Once there was a woman who was so grief-stricken by the death of her child. She wandered the streets carrying his lifeless body and asking strangers to help her bring him back to life. A sympathetic person accompanied her to meet the Buddha.

The Buddha told the woman: "Bring me some mustard seeds and I shall resurrect him. However, you must obtain them from a family who is a stranger to death."

The woman went on her way, desperately knocking from door to door. Alas, she returned in vain — for every family she had encountered had known death as well.

Finally, the woman realized the lesson that the Buddha wished to teach her. And that is: Sorrow is inescapable. If you expect to experience only happiness in your life, then you will suffer from frustration.

What are the four noble truths?

- **Suffering**

Suffering is universal. Everyone experiences it. For instance, death is inevitable. When we are ill, we feel miserable. Thus, to ask for a life devoid of disappointment would be unrealistic. The Buddha urges you to rise above self-deception and to really examine the way you live your life. The moment you wake up from your attitude of habitual denial, only then will you be able to follow the path to end suffering.

- **The Cause of Suffering**

We cause our own suffering. Take a look at the reasons for your own misery. How much of your unhappiness was brought about by greed? How much of it has been brought about by ignorance?

The problem with people is that they continue to seek happiness in all the wrong places. They pursue worldly pleasures that are harmful to their bodies, minds, and souls. In the end, satisfaction remains an elusive dream. For as long as you allow desire and attachment to control you, you shall never know true peace and contentment.

The Buddha teaches us to enjoy the pleasures of life without being greedy. You are urged to be sensitive to the needs of others, to take only what you need so that others will not be deprived of their share of the earth's resources.

- **The Termination of Suffering**

It is up to you to stop doing the things which cause suffering. The state where all suffering ceases to exist is called *Nirvana*. It is a perpetual state of peace and happiness.

According to the great Buddha, Nirvana is achieved through the extinction of desire. Nirvana is not synonymous with the concept of heaven. Instead, it is something which can be achieved right now, in this lifetime. Being Buddhist, you are called to follow a lifestyle which is free of selfishness and greed.

- **The Path Leading to the End of Suffering**

The secret to ending all suffering is for everyone to experience enlightenment. As previously mentioned, it was in his moment of awakening when the Buddha discovered the Middle Path.

To walk on this road, one must live the Noble Eightfold Path.

To check out the rest of the book, simply search for the title below on Amazon or go to:

bit.ly/Buddhism1

Buddhism For Beginners - *How To Go From Beginner To Monk And Master Your Mind*

201

Check Out My Other Popular Books

Below you'll find my other books that are popular on Amazon and Kindle as well. Simply enter the name of the books in the search bar on Amazon to check them out. Alternatively, you can visit my author page on Amazon to see other work done by me.

- *Michael Williams Author Page on Amazon*

- *Buddhism For Beginners* - *How To Go From Beginner To Monk And Master Your Mind*

- *ZEN: Beginner's Guide to Understanding & Practicing Zen Meditation to Become Present*

- ***Mindfulness for Beginners*** - *How to Live in The Present, Stress, and Anxiety Free*

- ***Mindfulness:*** *An Eight-Step Guide to Finding Peace and Removing Negativity From Your Everyday Life*

- *Mindfulness For Beginners - How to Relieve Stress and Anxiety Like a Buddhist Monk and Live In the Present Moment In Your Everyday Life*

- **Yoga For Men:** *Beginner's Step by Step Guide to a Stronger Body & Sharper Mind*

- **Chakras For Beginners** – *How to Awaken And Balance Chakras, Radiate Positive Energy And Heal Yourself*

- **Chakras for Beginners** - *Awaken Your Internal Energy and Learn to Radiate Positive Energy and Start Healing*